The Crusades and the Far-Right in the Twenty-First Century

Engaging the Crusades is a series of concise volumes (up to 50,000 words) which offer initial windows into the ways in which the crusades have been used in the last two centuries, demonstrating that the memory of the crusades is an important and emerging subject. Together, these studies suggest that the memory of the crusades, in the modern period, is a productive, exciting, and much-needed area of investigation.

This volume explores how crusading rhetoric, iconography, and historiography have been purposed by far-right, nationalist, and related groups in the recent past through case studies as varied as Brenton Tarrant, who killed 51 people at a mosque and Islamic centre in New Zealand in March 2019; a modern American 'military order' that uses memes to recruit members and spread its ideology; and the bestselling video game Assassin's Creed. As nationalist and far-right ideologies have gained adherents in Europe and the Americas, understanding how ideologues have misused the crusading past for their own ends is more important than ever.

The Crusades and the Far-Right in the Twenty-First Century is useful for all students and scholars interested in the intersection between the history of the crusades and far-right ideology in the modern age.

Charlotte Gauthier is Thornley Fellow at the Institute of Historical Research. Her research interests include the diplomatic and intellectual history of the later crusades, and the modern uses of crusading imagery and memory.

Engaging the Crusades: The Memory and Legacy of Crusading

Series Editors: *Jonathan Phillips and Mike Horswell, Royal Holloway, University of London, UK*

Engaging the Crusades is a series of volumes which offer initial windows into the ways in which the crusades have been used in the last two centuries; demonstrating that the memory of the crusades is an important and emerging subject. Together these studies suggest that the memory of the crusades, in the modern period, is a productive, exciting and much needed area of investigation.

In this series:

Playing the Crusades
Engaging the Crusades, Volume Five
Edited by Robert Houghton

Tales of the Crusaders – Remembering the Crusades in Britain
Engaging the Crusades, Volume Six
Elizabeth Siberry

The Modern Memory of the Military-Religious Orders
Engaging the Crusades, Volume Seven
Edited by Rory MacLellan

Nationalising the Crusades
Engaging the Crusades, Volume Eight
Edited by Mike Horswell

The Crusades and the Far-Right in the Twenty-First Century
Engaging the Crusades, Volume Nine
Edited by Charlotte Gauthier

For more information about this series, please visit: https://www.routledge.com/Engaging-the-Crusades/book-series/ETC

The Crusades and the Far-Right in the Twenty-First Century

Engaging the Crusades, Volume Nine

Edited by
Charlotte Gauthier

LONDON AND NEW YORK

First published 2025
by Routledge
4 Park Square, Milton Park, Abingdon, Oxon OX14 4RN

and by Routledge
605 Third Avenue, New York, NY 10158

Routledge is an imprint of the Taylor & Francis Group, an informa business

British Library Cataloguing-in-Publication Data
A catalogue record for this book is available from the British Library

ISBN: 9780367470432 (hbk)
ISBN: 9781032878577 (pbk)
ISBN: 9781003033035 (ebk)

DOI: 10.4324/9781003033035

Typeset in Times New Roman
by codeMantra

Contents

Acknowledgements

The editor would like to thank the contributors, whose patience and grace in engaging with the editorial process has made this volume possible. Profound gratitude also to the series editors, Jonathan Phillips and Mike Horswell, for their indefatigable encouragement and assistance on what for many reasons has been an unexpectedly long road. Thanks also to all at Routledge – not least Laura Pilsworth and Isabel Voice – for guiding this volume to publication.

Figures

Contributors

Joshua Call is Professor of English at Grand View University in Des Moines, Iowa. He is a former area chair of the Game Studies Area of the National Popular Culture Association and Managing Editor of the *Approaches to Digital Game Studies* series for Bloomsbury Press.

Andrew B.R. Elliott has published a range of articles and essays on historical film, television and video games from the classical world to the present. His latest book, *Medievalism and the Mass Media* (2017), explores the uses of the past in social media and mainstream news reporting.

Charlotte Gauthier is Thornley Fellow at the Institute of Historical Research. Her research interests include the diplomatic and intellectual history of the later crusades, the intersection of religious violence and nationhood, and the modern uses of crusading imagery and memory.

Thomas Lecaque is Associate Professor of History at Grand View University in Des Moines, Iowa. He studies apocalypticism and religious violence, from medieval to the modern day.

Rory MacLellan is Cataloguer and Manuscript Researcher at the British Library. He specialises in medieval religious history, especially the crusades and the military-religious orders. His first book, *Donations to the Knights Hospitaller in Britain and Ireland, 1291–1400*, is published by Routledge.

Francesca Petrizzo is Lecturer in Medieval History at the University of Glasgow. Her research focuses on practitioners of violence and their uses of the past to legitimise themselves between the central Middle Ages and medievalism in later ages.

Daniel Wollenberg is Associate Professor of English and Writing at the University of Tampa, Florida, specialising in medieval literature and culture. He has recently published articles on political medievalism on the far-right in the journal *postmedieval*.

Introduction

Contesting the 'Misuse' of History

Charlotte Gauthier

The crusades refuse to remain in the past. In recent decades, elements of crusading rhetoric, iconography, and historiography have been pressed into service by far-right, nationalist, and related groups – sometimes with tragic consequences. From the shield-carrying white supremacists of the 2017 'Unite the Right' rally in Charlottesville to 'Templar knight' and mass-murderer Anders Behring Breivik, self-styled 'crusaders' have often used a warped vision of the past as justification for antisocial or violent action in the present.[1] As nationalist and far-right ideologies have gained adherents in Europe and the Americas, and as the academy engages in a welcome debate over how the crusades are taught, understanding how ideologues have misused the crusading past for their own ends is more important than ever. This volume, as so much of the present debate on crusades pedagogy within the academy, is driven by two underlying questions: what motivates individuals on the far-right to appropriate the crusading past for ideological service in the present, and how might crusades historiography challenge or mitigate its own misuse?[2]

'Misuse' is, of course, a loaded term; such a charge implies that there is a normative or 'proper' use of history from which certain nationalist or far-right ideologues have deviated by weaving crusader medievalisms into their socio-political narratives. The question of the purpose and proper use of historiography is a very old one indeed, and it is not within the scope of this introduction to analyse the various arguments advanced by scholars over the past century.[3] In any case, these arguments relate to the writing of history *by historians*, while those on the far-right who employ crusader medievalisms for their social and political purposes are most often not historians, either by training or by trade. Their purpose is not to engage with historiography per se, but rather to construct an imagined past in service of a desired future. As Andrew B.R. Elliott notes, such usage of history 'often rejects the past altogether in the service of a shared cultural repository of symbols'.[4] Fundamental to understanding the 'misuse' of history as examined in the essays in this book therefore is a brief exploration of the idea of history as symbol or locus of memory and a foundation for nationhood or shared culture.[5]

DOI: 10.4324/9781003033035-1

In a 1972 essay on 'The Social Function of the Past', Eric Hobsbawm argued that nationalist movements, 'because their objectives are historically unprecedented, nevertheless insist on defining them to a greater or lesser extent in historical terms and actually attempt to realize parts of this fictitious history'.[6] Hobsbawm quoted Ernest Renan, who argued in his seminal 1882 essay 'What is a Nation? (Qu'est-ce qu'une nation?)' that 'The act of forgetting, I would even say, historical error, is an essential factor in the creation of a nation, which is why progress in historical studies often constitutes a danger for nationality'.[7] Renan was speaking of the nation-state, which he defined as a 'spiritual principle' constituted of 'the possession in common of a rich legacy of memories' and 'present consent, the desire to live together, the will to perpetuate the value of the heritage that one has received in an undivided form',[8] but the principle can be argued to be true for any (would-be) political or social movement in almost any era. Indeed, historical error is now no less essential to constructing a 'common legacy of memory' to provide the rationale for action in the present than it has ever been.[9]

The rise of the internet with its disintermediation of former gatekeepers (e.g., the mainstream press, the academy, and governments) has led the creation of such narratives to accelerate and to take on a fragmented character. The internet cannot create physical nation-states, but Renan's 'will to perpetuate the value of the heritage that one has received in an undivided form' persists in the rhetoric of modern-day nationalists and far-right figures who speak about a notional shared 'Western' history and cultural heritage that has in reality been cobbled together by many hands ('crowdsourced' and 'remixed', in internet parlance) from numerous heterogeneous sources, as the essays in this book explore. The internet provides an ideal platform for the sort of selective historical forgetfulness necessary to construct a shared set of historical symbols that will hold emergent distributed groups (such as those porous and frangible groups found on internet message boards, social media sites, or gaming platforms) together for a time around a certain political or social goal. There need be very little political or ideological coherence in these shared mythologies in order for them to be effective, and little if any verifiable historicity.[10] Elliott has suggested that the production of these symbols – or rather, of the transformation of the Middle Ages from a historical period into a 'site of identity, a point of identification or an ideological weapon' – runs in three phases. The first is 'historical expropriation [...] the mode through which and in which medieval objects and concepts are invoked in the post-medieval period'. The second phase is 'repetition and retransmission [...] which "flattens out" the meaning and allows new meanings and significance to be established'. The third is 'assimilation, transmission, or modification', whereby medievalisms are coupled with modern ideologies and reified into symbols utterly disconnected from their original medieval meaning and context.[11] When we speak of the 'misuse' or 'appropriation' of history, therefore, we speak of this process.

This is not meant to imply that figures such as Brenton Tarrant or Anders Behring Breivik or Andrew J. Baalman and Alexis Bugnolo are leaders of actual mass social or political movements, let alone nation-states – far from it. There is a danger of seeming to do their intellectual work for them by connecting certain features of their writings or actions into a coherent ideological whole, which has little basis in evidence. Nevertheless, it is highly interesting and relevant in light of the argument made above that each of these individuals – and others mentioned in the following chapters – claims (albeit untruthfully) to be a member of an organised movement. Likewise, when we speak of the 'far-right' or 'alt-right', there is a danger of seeming to reify those concepts into a coherent political movement, rather than examining them as loose constellations of ideologies. When we use the term 'far-right', we mean nothing more than a heterogenous collection of individuals professing a set of political beliefs that include ultra-nationalist, reactionary, illiberal, authoritarian, and often racist and/or nativist tendencies.[12] The 'alt-right' was a far-right internet sub-culture that grew up around the 2016 US presidential election, consisting of loosely affiliated white supremacists who opposed some combination of mainstream conservatism, immigration, social justice, Islam, feminism, and 'political correctness'.[13]

The following essays examine the multifarious ways in which individuals and self-described groups on the far-right have engaged with – or avoided – crusades historiography in the twenty-first century in order to transmute the contingent facts of history into both a shared memory of the past, and a licence for action (even violent action) in the present. Francesca Petrizzo demonstrates the disconnect between popular perceptions of the First Crusade and the academic debate surrounding it through the lens of Brenton Tarrant's valorisation of Bohemond I of Antioch, whose name he engraved on the weapons with which he killed 51 people at a mosque and Islamic centre in New Zealand in March 2019. Rory MacLellan examines the 'Ordo Catholicus Militaris' – a US-based modern 'military order' – arguing that it forgoes the pop culture references and memes so popular with other neo-crusaders and instead uses often obscure aspects of medieval history to create a sense of authenticity as a 'genuine' military order to recruit members and spread its ideology. Andrew B.R. Elliott explores how the UK's right-wing populist *Daily Express* newspaper uses the 'little crusader' motif to sell its vision of Brexit as a return to a halcyon past. Daniel Wollenberg explores the use of chivalric and crusading rhetoric and imagery by neo-Confederates in the American Deep South, arguing that for neo-Confederate thought, the Civil War plays a similar role that the crusades have played for the far and extreme right in the US, Europe, and Australia. Joshua Call and Thomas Lecaque examine the portrayal of the crusades in the bestselling video game *Assassin's Creed*, which, they argue, played an important role in the genesis of alt-right game spaces, which then gave birth to the 'GamerGate' controversy and contemporary neo-fascist groups.

What ties these case studies together is the construction by individuals or small groups of a collective memory and identity using a fictionalised and idealised version of the crusading past. This brings us full-circle to the second of the two questions posed at the beginning of this introduction: can and should scholars respond to far-right usage of crusader medievalisms to inspire violence or antisocial behaviour? In posing this question, there is a danger of scholars taking unjustified responsibility for the ways in which historiography is (mis)used. Historians can neither determine nor control how their work is received or employed by others once it is made available in the public sphere. This does not absolve them from the need to act, however: very much under the historian's control are the ways in which they themselves write, speak, and teach about the past.

In recent years, the academy and some elements of mass media have begun to reconsider the ways in which they communicate complex or contested history to both students and the general public.[14] Susanna Throop has written of the importance of 'working intentionally' – that is, 'undertak[ing] self-reflection, [...] actively consider[ing] both the ethics and the limits of history, [...] engag[ing] the public in the complexity of history, and [...] acknowledg[ing] the interconnections between the teaching and writing of history and its public understanding'.[15] By understanding the political, social, and cultural contexts into which they are writing, and communicating accordingly – in short, by equipping those whom they address to think and converse about the past in informed ways – the historian might provide an alternative to bad-faith distortions of the past put forward in service of far-right ideology in the present.[16] Despite the erosion of 'legacy' media platforms and the numerous present difficulties faced by the academy, historians retain a certain public authority to interpret the past. Let us do so – and help others to do so – in a way that centres criticality, context, and awareness.

Bibliography

Primary

Putin, Vladimir. 'On the Historical Unity of Russians and Ukrainians', 12 July 2021. https://web.archive.org/web/20220310004907/http://en.kremlin.ru/events/president/news/66181

Secondary

Bauer, A.J. 'The Alternative Historiography of the Alt-Right: Conservative Historical Subjectivity from the Tea Party to Trump'. In *Far-Right Revisionism and the End of History: Alt/Histories*, ed. Louie Dean Valencia-García. Abingdon: Routledge, 2020, pp. 121–38.

Berlin, Isaiah. 'The Concept of Scientific History' and 'The Hedgehog and the Fox'. In *The Proper Study of Mankind*, ed. Henry Hardy and Roger Hausheer. London: Vintage Books, 2013, pp. 17–58, 436–98.

Bloch, Marc. *The Historian's Craft*, trans. Peter Putman. Manchester: Manchester University Press, 2002.

Carr, E.H. *What Is History?* Basingstoke: Palgrave Macmillan, 2008.

Cotts, John D. 'The Academic Historiography of the Crusades and the Twenty-First Century Debate on Religious Violence'. *International Journal of Military History and Historiography* 41.2 (2020), pp. 343–76.

Elliott, Andrew B.R. *Medievalism, Politics and Mass Media: Appropriating the Middle Ages in the Twenty-First Century*, *Medievalism*, 10. Woodbridge: D.S. Brewer, 2017.

Elton, G.R. *The Practice of History*. London: Fontana Press, 1987.

Hobsbawm, Eric. 'The Social Function of the Past: Some Questions'. *Past and Present* 55.1 (1972), pp. 3–17.

Koch, Ariel. 'The New Crusaders: Contemporary Extreme Right Symbolism and Rhetoric'. *Perspectives on Terrorism* 11.5 (2017), pp. 13–24.

Kogod, Theo. '*Assassin's Creed Valhalla:* How Literal Nazis Appropriate Viking Video Games'. CBR.com, 19 January 2021. https://web.archive.org/web/20240413133222/https://www.cbr.com/assassins-creed-valhalla-nazi-appropriation/.

Pirro, Andrea L.P. 'Far Right: The Significance of an Umbrella Concept'. *Nations and Nationalism* 29.1 (2023), pp. 101–12.

Popper, Karl. *The Poverty of Historicism*. London: Routledge, 2002.

Ramsay, Gilbert. *Jihadi Culture on the World Wide Web*. New York: Bloomsbury Academic, 2013.

Renan, Ernest. 'What Is a Nation?? (Qu'est-ce qu'une nation?, 1882)'. In *What Is a Nation? And Other Political Writings*, ed. M.F.N. Giglioli. New York: Columbia University Press, 2018, pp. 247–63.

Skottki, Kristin. 'The Dead, the Revived, and the Re-created Pasts: "Structural Amnesia" in Representations of Crusade History'. In *Perceptions of the Crusades from the Nineteenth to the Twenty-First Century*, ed. Mike Horswell and Jonathan Phillips, Engaging the Crusades, 1. Abingdon: Routledge, 2018, pp. 107–32.

Tait, Joshua. 'What Was the Alt-Right?'. *Tablet*, 11 August 2023. https://web.archive.org/web/20240105224341/https://www.tabletmag.com/sections/news/articles/what-was-alt-right/.

Throop, Susanna. 'Engaging the Crusades in Context: Reflections on the Ethics of Historical Work'. In *The Crusades in the Modern World*, ed. Mike Horswell and Akil N. Awan, Engaging the Crusades, 2. Abingdon: Routledge, 2020, pp. 129–45.

Whitaker, Cord. 'The Problem of Alt-Right Medievalist White Supremacy, and Its Black Medievalist Answer'. In *Far-Right Revisionism and the End of History: Alt / Histories*, ed. Louie Dean Valencia-García, Routledge Approaches to History, 37. New York: Routledge Taylor & Francis Group, 2020, pp. 159–76.

Notes

1 Ariel Koch, 'The New Crusaders: Contemporary Extreme Right Symbolism and Rhetoric', *Perspectives on Terrorism*, 11.5 (2017), 13–24.

2 See, e.g., A.J. Bauer, 'The Alternative Historiography of the Alt-Right: Conservative Historical Subjectivity from the Tea Party to Trump', in *Far-Right Revisionism and the End of History: Alt/Histories*, ed. Louie Dean Valencia-García (Abingdon, 2020), pp. 121–38; Cord Whitaker, 'The Problem of Alt-Right Medievalist White Supremacy, and Its Black Medievalist Answer', in *Far-Right Revisionism and the End of History: Alt / Histories*, ed. Louie Dean Valencia-García, 37 (New York, 2020), pp. 159–76.

3 Or indeed over the past few millennia; Marc Bloch begins his discussion of the purpose and methods of historical analysis by quoting the similar opinions of Leopold von Ranke and Herodotus: Marc Bloch, *The Historian's Craft*, trans. Peter Putman (Manchester, 2002), p. 114. For some contrasting twentieth-century voices in this debate, see Isaiah Berlin, 'The Concept of Scientific History' and 'The Hedgehog and the Fox', in *The Proper Study of Mankind* (London, 2013), pp. 17–58, 436–98; Bloch, *The Historian's Craft*; E.H. Carr, *What Is History?* (Basingstoke, 2008); G.R. Elton, *The Practice of History* (London, 1987); Karl Popper, *The Poverty of Historicism* (London, 2002).

4 Andrew B.R. Elliott, *Medievalism, Politics and Mass Media: Appropriating the Middle Ages in the Twenty-First Century* (Woodbridge, 2017), p. 4.

5 For a longer and more detailed consideration, see Kristin Skottki, 'The Dead, the Revived, and the Re-created Pasts: "Structural Amnesia" in Representations of Crusade History', in *Perceptions of the Crusades from the Nineteenth to the Twenty-First Century: Engaging the Crusades, Volume One*, ed. Mike Horswell and Jonathan Phillips (Abingdon, 2018), pp. 107–32.

6 Eric Hobsbawm, 'The Social Function of the Past: Some Questions', *Past and Present*, 55.1 (1972), p. 9.

7 Ernest Renan, 'What Is a Nation?? (Qu'est-ce qu'une nation?, 1882)', in *What Is a Nation? And Other Political Writings*, ed. M.F.N. Giglioli (Columbia University Press, 2018), p. 251.

8 Renan, 'What Is a Nation?', p. 261.

9 Two more notorious recent examples of the fictionalisation of history for political purposes by nationalist figures include Donald Trump's slogan 'Make America Great Again' – which implies a halcyon past that Trump promises to re-create for his supporters – and Vladimir Putin's July 2021 essay 'On the Historical Unity of Russians and Ukrainians', which presaged the Russian invasion of Ukraine in spring 2022, in which he rewrites the history of Kievan Rus to bolster Russia's claims to ownership of Ukraine whilst simultaneously criticising the leadership of Ukraine for 'mythologiz[ing] and rewrit[ing] history' in the service of their own geopolitical goals <https://web.archive.org/web/20220310004907/http://en.kremlin.ru/events/president/news/66181> [accessed 6 May 2024].

10 Gilbert Ramsay, *Jihadi Culture on the World Wide Web* (New York, 2013), chap. 7.

11 Elliott, *Medievalism*, p. 6.

12 Andrea L.P. Pirro, 'Far Right: The Significance of an Umbrella Concept', *Nations and Nationalism*, 29.1 (2023), 101–12.

13 For an examination of the 'alt-right' phenomenon and its evanescence, see Joshua Tait, 'What Was the Alt-Right?', *Tablet*, 11 August 2023 <https://web.archive.org/web/20240105224341/https://www.tabletmag.com/sections/news/articles/what-was-alt-right> [accessed 6 May 2024].

14 Ubisoft, maker of the *Assassin's Creed* games franchise, has removed some symbolism frequently appropriated by white supremacists from its games: Theo Kogod, '*Assassin's Creed Valhalla:* How Literal Nazis Appropriate Viking Video Games', CBR.com, 19 January 2021 <https://web.archive.org/web/20240413133222/https://www.cbr.com/assassins-creed-valhalla-nazi-appropriation/> [accessed 6 May 2024]. However, see Lecaque and Call's chapter in this volume.

15 Susanna Throop, 'Engaging the Crusades in Context: Reflections on the Ethics of Historical Work', in *The Crusades in the Modern World: Engaging the Crusades, Volume Two*, ed. Mike Horswell and Akil N. Awan (Abingdon, 2020), pp. 129–45.

16 For an example of such awareness in practice, see John D. Cotts, 'The Academic Historiography of the Crusades and the Twenty-First Century Debate on Religious Violence', *International Journal of Military History and Historiography*, 41.2 (2020), 343–76.

1 'Bad Crusader'

Bohemond, the Scholars, and the Christchurch Shooter[1]

Francesca Petrizzo

On 15 March 2019, during the Muslim Friday prayer in the early afternoon, two consecutive attacks took place in the Al Noor Mosque and the Linwood Islamic Centre in the city of Christchurch, Aotearoa New Zealand.[2] A shooter opened fire on the faithful gathered in worship, killing 51 and wounding 49. Brenton Tarrant, a 28-year-old white Australian national, was charged with the attacks.[3] After an initial not-guilty plea, in March 2020, Tarrant pleaded guilty to 51 charges of murder, 40 charges of attempted murder, and one charge of engaging in a terrorist act, and was convicted and later sentenced to life in prison without parole.[4] The consequences of the attack, with its dramatically high victim count, had far-ranging repercussions on New Zealand legislation, its internal societal discourse, and international assessments of the reach and spread of white supremacist and Islamophobic terrorism. The reach and aftershocks of the attack were made wider by the shooter's thorough use of the internet to broadcast his actions. The Al Noor Mosque attack was livestreamed via Facebook, and the video immediately shared to other platforms; Tarrant wrote and published online a manifesto, which was sent, among others, to the New Zealand Prime Minister's office shortly before the attack.[5] Tarrant displayed a strategic usage of internet memes and mottoes to connect with his audience, for instance, shouting 'Subscribe to PewDiePie' at the end of his livestreamed attack, evoking the popular gaming YouTuber.[6] The references Tarrant used varied, from the historical to the contemporary, from the niche to the mainstream, painting a precise and detailed picture of the framework with which he sought to underpin his act. This chapter focuses on one particular aspect of the intertextual and iconographical web the shooter inscribed his attack into: the use of crusader imagery in order to justify and celebrate his massacre of Muslim civilians.

Among the preparations made to advertise his actions, Tarrant shared on Twitter (now 'X') a number of pictures of his gun magazines, displaying the ammunition he would use to commit the attack.[7] Written in white paint on the polymer were the names of numerous historical figures, united by having been successful Christian fighters against Muslims in Europe and the Mediterranean, in the medieval and early modern era. Among the names was that

DOI: 10.4324/9781003033035-2

of Bohemond I of Antioch, a Southern Italian Norman and one of the leaders of the First Crusade, who featured prominently in the conquest of Antioch from the Seljuk Turks in 1098. This chapter will focus on how the use of Bohemond's name in particular highlights a disconnect between the popular perception of the crusader movement and the historiographical debate, and offers us further insight into the task of the scholars in engaging public perceptions of the crusader movement, and our difficulty discerning and combating the potential for its appropriation by the far-right. Bohemond, long and nearly universally perceived by scholars as a 'bad crusader' who hijacked the First Crusade in order to pursue his own expansionistic policy against the Byzantine Empire, would seem at first an odd fit within the propaganda efforts of Tarrant in pursuit of crusader 'legitimacy' for his attack. However, as I will show in this chapter, closer attention to the ways Bohemond's figure has been perceived and celebrated help us in fact shed light as to the difficulty and the necessity of engaging more closely with the ways the medieval past is attractive to the far-right for use as propaganda, and how experts of a topic may become blind to its inherent potential for destructiveness through their own bias (in my case, my perspective as a white scholar closely involved with the research which makes Bohemond seem like an unlikely model for the use of white supremacist terrorists as propaganda). While, as Ibrahim Al-Marashi has pointed out, Tarrant suffered from 'common historical delusions' in his flattened reading of the medieval past, still he was seizing on aspects of it which scholars should be alert to, and address explicitly, as I will show here.[8]

To begin, Tarrant's invocation of the medieval past to justify his act places him in a line of ideologically similar agents. The 2011 attack by Norwegian white supremacist Anders Breivik at the Utøya summer camp was underpinned by a detailed manifesto, which sought to frame his gesture as one in defence of Europe, which Breivik claimed to be threatened by multiculturalism and progressiveness, and it evoked the medieval past as an idealised ideological and societal moment to which the attacker claimed Europe should return.[9] The August 2017 'Unite the Right' rally in Charlottesville, Virginia, which led to violence and saw one dead, featured numerous instances of the use of medieval imagery by members of the alt-right.[10] Marchers carried shields, helms, and banners which displayed medieval or medieval-inspired symbols and emblems, together with other far-right symbols such as confederate battle flags and Nazi regalia.[11] The clear claim the alt-right movement was making to the Middle Ages was immediately confronted in academia itself, through engagement with the issues of teaching, studying, and popularising the Middle Ages in the twenty-first century.[12] It is therefore in many ways unsurprising that Tarrant should have chosen to evoke Christian holy war when framing his attack on the Christchurch Muslim community: the evocation of an imagined medieval past as the idealised *locus* of a common, unchallenged, white European identity has permeated several aspects of alt-right propaganda, rallying around poles such as the Viking era, the crusades, and the wider framework of medieval Western European Christianity.[13]

Tarrant's closest interest seems to have lain with the Muslim-Christian conflict on Europe's Eastern area, from the Balkans to Russia via Romania, Bulgaria, and Poland, focusing most insistently on the wars against the Ottoman Empire. He appears to have been especially interested in the Adriatic area, quoting the names of medieval, early modern and modern military leaders from Montenegro, Serbia and Venice, with special interest in the 1570 Battle of Lepanto.[14] He also referenced Hungary, with Szilágyi Mihály (*c.*1400–60), who also defended Belgrade from Ottoman attack in 1456, bringing us back to the Adriatic area. In comparison, references to the non-Eastern European, non-Ottoman conflict are rarer: we can only count among them Charles Martel (*c.*688–741), and Pelagius of Asturias (*c.*685–737), who fought the Iberian Muslims, and a few references to the crusades, with Bohemond, Gaston of Béarn (*d.*1130), and the siege of Acre (1189).[15]

When referencing the modern era, Tarrant seems to have similarly looked to Eastern Europe. With Dmitry Senyavin (1763–1831), the Battle of Kagul (1770), the Battle of the Shipka Pass (1877), and Iosif Gurko (1828–1901), he referenced the Russo-Turkish wars, and with Edward Codrington (1770–1851) the Greek war of independence from the Ottomans. Tarrant also wrote in the names of several contemporary shooters who carried out attacks against Muslims, or perceived non-European 'others': next to Alexandre Bissonette, perpetrator of the January 2017 Quebec City Mosque shooting which killed six, he also wrote in the name of much lesser-known Luca Traini, who in February 2017 in Macerata, Italy, carried out an attack which injured six immigrants of colour.[16] As highlighted by political scientist Jasmin Mujanović, Tarrant also referenced 1990s Serbian nationalist propaganda by repeatedly saying 'Remove kebab', an anti-Bosnian, anti-Muslim slogan used during the Balkan genocide, something not usually well-known among Western far-right members.[17] Tarrant's interest in Eastern European history and anti-Muslim movements there is underscored by his ties to the Austrian far-right: after making a substantial donation to Austrian party Identitäre Bewegung Österreichs (IBÖ), Tarrant appeared to have corresponded in a friendly manner with its leader, Martin Sellner.[18] The Polish special services investigated Tarrant's suggestion that the anti-Muslim movement might begin from Poland, which he claimed to have visited, as did officials in Turkey, Greece, and Bulgaria, through which he had travelled.[19] The manifesto was sold in book form in Ukraine.[20]

Within this framework, Tarrant's interest in the crusades in the Holy Land seems to have been much more cursory: he referenced only two crusaders, and, interestingly, not explicitly the conquest of Jerusalem (1099), but rather the siege of Acre. Tarrant eschewed references to the most popular and best-known representatives of the crusader movement; while the siege of Acre is well-known, Tarrant did not bring up one of the warriors famous for it, England's ruler, Richard the Lionheart. The Third Crusade has generally enjoyed the most extensive fictional representation in the modern era, with numerous book series and one major Hollywood film (*Kingdom of Heaven*, 2005), which would seem to make it a more immediate reference for a general public, but Tarrant apparently was not interested in engaging at length with it.[21] He only referenced the Templars, briefly, in his manifesto.[22] Given his interests in Eastern Europe, he might also have been expected to engage with the Teutonic Order, whose extensive campaigns in the Baltic extended the reach of Christian Europe into new areas, but he did not.[23]

Tarrant appears to have been keen to present an image of the war waged against Muslims in Europe as a defensive one. By referencing the sieges of Vienna and Belgrade, Charles Martel, the conquest of Cyprus, and the struggles for independence from the Ottomans of Greece, Montenegro, and Serbia, Tarrant clearly wished to frame his act as one of resistance against perceived aggression, attempting to equate the Muslim civilians he targeted with the military strength of the Ottoman Empire, in line with the Islamophobia spread throughout the War on Terror. In this sense, therefore, the siege of Acre fits into this theme more easily than the successful conquest of Jerusalem by the First Crusade would: instead of focusing on the conquest of the holy city, which was notoriously followed by the slaughter of its inhabitants, Tarrant seemingly referenced the re-taking of Acre from the forces of Salah-ad-Din, who had recently conquered it. This seeming shying away from Jerusalem, however, is complicated by the references to Gaston of Béarn, a minor leader of the First Crusade. Together with Tancred, according to the *Gesta Francorum*, Gaston was the sole crusader to attempt to spare civilians during the massacre in Jerusalem, a gesture of seeming mercy wholly out of place with contemporary crusader practice.[24] While it is only the *Gesta* which mentions Gaston doing so, the reaction of other chroniclers to Tancred's gesture goes a long way in telling us how unpopular the action was: Albert of Aachen has the leader of the crusaders, Godfrey of Bouillon, telling off the younger warrior for 'sloth, greed or mercy', while two of the chroniclers most sympathetic to Tancred, William of Tyre and Ralph of Caen, do not mention the gesture at all.[25]

Tarrant, however, may have seized on Gaston de Béarn, a crusader neither well-known nor often featured in popular media, and he may indeed have learnt of him, through another connection: the fact that after the First Crusade, Gaston took part in the Christian campaigns against the Muslims in Spain, and died near Valencia in 1130.[26] Gaston's origins in Béarn, on the French side of the Pyrenees and thus in close proximity and cooperation with Aragón, chimes with Tancred's probable service in Sicily at the end of his great-uncle Roger's conquest of it from the Muslims, making them the two crusaders most likely to have a more complex and layered relationship with the non-Christian inhabitants of Jerusalem. Nonetheless, looked at from the point of view of Tarrant's interests, Gaston of Béarn becomes an emblematic warrior for European 'Christendom': someone who had successfully fought the Muslims from one end of the Mediterranean to the other, both a conqueror of Jerusalem and a participant in the 'Reconquista' (a loaded term and concept, still worryingly popular).[27] Spain is the non-Eastern European country which features most often on Tarrant's ammunition, as seen above: one of the names present on the weapons is that of Josué Estébanez, a Spanish neo-Nazi who in 2007 killed an anti-fascist protestor.[28] Already, we can see how Tarrant's choices in fact follow an internal logic, and one which shows up the limits of the academic debate in tackling it. As Kristin Skottki has pointed out, 'it seems odd to expect terrorist organisations [...] to engage with history like a research centre': academic approaches to deconstruction of such uses of history are ineffective if they insist on imposing a supposedly 'truthful' academic lens onto the medievalist practice of radical agents (whose medievalist perceptions, in turn, as Skottki rightfully points out, are often borrowed by now outdated but once very academically current interpretations).[29]

Moreover, unlike Gaston, Bohemond was, in his own time, one of the best-known crusaders, and a notorious character throughout Europe.[30] A son of Robert Guiscard, Norman conqueror of the Italian South and duke of Apulia, Bohemond was second-in-command for his father Robert during the latter's second campaign against the Byzantine Empire.[31] At the beginning of the First Crusade, Bohemond had been besieging the town of Amalfi alongside his uncle Count Roger (and, significantly, the latter's Sicilian Muslim soldiers).[32] Bohemond, however, chose to immediately begin recruiting Southern Italian knights and prepare to join the expedition to Jerusalem, disrupting Roger's campaign. Bohemond was, in turn, the Byzantine Emperor Alexios' closest interlocutor among the Western leaders, and a man to watch for the Byzantines.[33] It was at the siege of Antioch (1097–98) that Bohemond distinguished himself: the *de facto* leader of the crusader contingent, Bohemond was instrumental in the taking of the city, persuading one of its inhabitants, Firuz, to betray it to the crusaders. Through sleight of hand and obstinacy, Bohemond persuaded the other crusaders to leave him in charge of Antioch as they marched on to Jerusalem, instead of returning the city to the emperor as promised. Bohemond did not travel to the holy places until after the conquest.

After an eventful few years which involved further campaigning on the edge of the newborn Latin Kingdom of Jerusalem and a stint in captivity, in 1105, Bohemond headed back West, with the intention of raising an anti-Byzantine crusade. His notoriety served him well: it may have been Bohemond who hawked the original text of the *Gesta Francorum* around Europe.[34] Henry I of England barred him from setting foot in Britain, seemingly afraid Bohemond would entice his nobility on crusade.[35] In France, Bohemond fulfilled and exceeded his ambitions: not only did he obtain the backing he wanted for his expedition, but he arranged royal marriages to King Phillip's daughters, Constance and Cecile, for himself and Tancred. His final campaign against the Byzantines, however, was a disaster. Stranded in the middle of the Balkans, his army weakened by hunger and disease, Bohemond had to surrender, and in 1108 he acknowledged imperial overlordship over the principality he had founded in Antioch. When Bohemond died in Southern Italy in 1111, he was very much a defeated man, who had had to withdraw back to the lands obtained from his brother.

Bohemond's life and career, with their dramatic reversals of fortunes and impossibly ambitious plans, sketch him out as a striking man, considered powerfully charismatic by his own contemporaries. But if Bohemond cast a long shadow in his own time, none of the characteristics that made him an attractive figure to those who surrounded him seem to speak much of his interest in the crusade as a holy war. Consistently, Bohemond prioritised his inroads into Byzantine territories over the stated goals of the crusade: entrenching himself in Antioch only to emerge to seek to engage the Byzantines again, and significantly stripping it of resources as he left, which threw the principality into a crisis from which Tancred struggled hard to lift it.[36] Modern historians have characterised him accordingly, as the 'wily son of a notoriously wily father', who fought Byzantium, first and foremost, all his life.[37] Nor was Bohemond praised in the Middle Ages for his religious character or piety; unlike Tancred, who enjoyed a long heyday of popularity as a model of chivalry, he was not known as a model of knightly virtue.[38] Steven Runciman, whose history of the crusades remains enduringly influential, and easily accessible to the public, acknowledged Bohemond's personal charisma but damned his unscrupulous ambition.[39] In his popular 1964 novel *Count Bohemond*, Alfred Duggan portrayed his protagonist as a cosmopolitan, worldly man, well-aware of the material advantages of waging holy war, archly amused by his nephew Tancred, who in the novel embodies a form of bigoted, intolerant Christianity.[40] Laverne Gay, whose literary writing was thoroughly seasoned with documentary research, wrote Bohemond as a romantic hero, somewhat disillusioned but always dashing, not as a religious leader.[41] Even bucking past problematic moralistic assessments of crusaders as 'good' role models, historian Christopher Tyerman could at best say that Bohemond was 'no worse than the others': a marked improvement from David Douglas, who had called both Bohemond and Tancred 'personally repellent', but one which still clearly remains aware of the mistrust that reliably accompanies Bohemond in the sources.[42] Bohemond was perceived in his own time as a famous crusader, but one whose interests rested first and foremost with himself, and modern historiography has agreed with this assessment.

Why, then, was his name written on Tarrant's ammunition magazines?

Firstly, there is geography. As we have seen, Tarrant showed himself most interested in the Balkans and Eastern Europe. A man with lands in Apulia, who had fought in the Balkans with his father, and had crossed there on his way to Constantinople, Bohemond spent much of his life and career in the Adriatic environment Tarrant seems to have been engrossed with. Bohemond, an Adriatic Norman with lifelong interests in the Balkans, may have looked to

Tarrant the ideal earlier counterpart of the Montenegrin and Serbian warriors he so plentifully cited. At the same time, the point remains that Bohemond, as we have shown, was most interested in fighting the Byzantines, and not the Muslims; he was not, like Gaston of Béarn, a warrior active on several edges of the Muslim-Christian conflict at once. We have no evidence Bohemond ever took part in his uncle Roger's campaigns against the Muslims of Sicily; indeed, the evidence we have for him before the First Crusade shows him fighting alongside Sicilian Muslims, not against them. If Gaston's act of seeming mercy in sparing the civilians in the Temple may look like tolerance, it also needs to be laid next to a consistent career as a fighter of non-Christians. But for Bohemond, there had been no such consistency. What then made him an appealing model?

The answer may lay in a crucial aspect of Bohemond's representation: his reputation as a formidable warrior and leader of men. A fundamental part of Bohemond's appeal always rested in his ability to lead: it is to his quality in both negotiating with his peers and winning followers that much of the qualified praise which surrounds him in the chronicles of the First Crusade rests. We have seen how threatened even kings could feel by him, and how successfully he had disrupted his uncle Roger's campaign. The fall of Antioch is credited to his personal relationship with the Antiochene Firuz, whom he persuaded to let the Christians into the walls.[43] An impressive quality seems to have accompanied Bohemond, one such as to evoke respect, fear, and to inspire men to follow him. What this has translated into is a profound interest in Bohemond's perceived qualities as a general and military commander. Bohemond has long been ranked among the most memorable warriors of the Middle Ages: all accounts of his life acknowledge what Douglas termed his 'intense ability'.[44] His career is amply documented: we have detailed descriptions of Bohemond's time fighting with guerrilla methods on behalf of his father Guiscard; of Bohemond's obstinate holding out against his brother; of his effective command of the crusader forces across Asia Minor; of his effective leadership of the lengthy, traumatic siege of Antioch.[45] Anna Komnene acknowledged the magnitude of the threat presented by Bohemond to the Byzantine Empire, the defeat of such a man a substantial achievement for her father.[46]

The quantity of detail available for Bohemond's military activity tells us both that his own contemporaries were impressed by it, and goes a long way to explain the enduring interest in it by military historians. It is unsurprising that the first biography in English of Bohemond in more than a hundred years should come from a specialist of Norman and Byzantine military history.[47] Bestselling historian Peter Frankopan's work on the First Crusade recognised Bohemond as a shrewd, dangerous, tremendously effective operator, even when thoroughly condemning his double-crossing of Alexios.[48] If all scholars seem to agree that Bohemond was less than invested in dedicating his warrior skills to the crusader cause, they still concur with medieval chroniclers that those skills were impressive. The information has not been lost on the wider public. YouTube channel *Real Crusades History*, whose outlook on the crusades is not critical, invited an expert scholar on the history of Antioch to discuss Bohemond's controversial career and the founding of the principality of Antioch in a scholarly manner; but they also made several videos examining in depth and celebrating Bohemond's military achievements from a strategic standpoint.[49] While the well-subscribed channel *History Time* dedicated far more attention to Tancred than to Bohemond in their documentaries, it was to Bohemond's military ability that they most insistently referred in their analysis, once more propagating the view of Bohemond as a good leader.[50]

Here, we find the key to why Bohemond, the 'bad crusader' with a Byzantine agenda and scarce interest in taking or defending Jerusalem, was cited on the weapons of the Christchurch shooter. Whatever reason he may have had to do so, Bohemond was ultimately an Adriatic Christian warrior who had inflicted a profound defeat on the Seljuk Turks, at least nominally as part of a crusader expedition. As such, he fits in entirely with Tarrant's other models: Christian men who had fought Muslims, usually Turks, in Eastern Europe and Western Asia, and through whose successful military careers Tarrant sought to justify his own attack on unarmed Muslim civilians in New Zealand. In this sense, historians' evaluation of Bohemond's effective investment in the crusade's ideological aspects becomes less important than the victories he won while at least nominally wearing the cross, and of the way his personal charisma impressed those victories on both his contemporaries, and those who followed. As pointed out by Adam Bishop, if on the one hand white supremacists' perceptions of the crusader movement are simplistic, on the other, they seize on what was undoubtedly a fundamental element of it: armed opposition between Christians and Muslims.[51] If it can be easily shown that a persuasive and even popular case for Bohemond's lack of investment in ideologically motivated war against Muslims exists, it is just as easy to see why someone like Tarrant, interested in choosing symbols for what he wanted to present as his personal 'crusade', could seize on his well-known military prowess as a signifier of his own agenda.

Nor is the issue of claiming the crusader identity confined to the alt-right; popular readings of the crusades can seem just as sharply divorced from the academic dialogue, as shown by another event connected to the Christchurch shooting. Part of the effort to examine what government and society could do to foster a safer and more welcoming environment for their Muslim community involved Christchurch's local rugby team, a hugely successful club known as the Crusaders. The team had long leant into the medievalism evoked by their name: their logo represented a cross-bearing knight, while their matches were often preceded by re-enactors parading on the pitch on horse, in chainmail and cross-emblazoned surcoats, wielding swords, and one of their past campaigns had carried the slogan 'join the crusade'.[52] Unsurprisingly, a debate was opened as to whether the team should change its name in the wake of the attacks, forsaking its explicit associations to medieval holy war. The debate was made more complex by the fondness for the team displayed by its fans, many of whom belonged to the same Muslim community that had been so tragically targeted.[53] Ultimately, a seeming compromise was found when the team chose to abandon its old logo and the medievalist displays, but kept the name, with chief executive Colin Mansbridge announcing that: 'It was decided that no name better represented the club's commitment to living its values – crusading for social improvement and inclusiveness, and crusading with heart for our community and for each other'.[54] The team, thus, was attempting to separate the medievalist heritage they were clearly and explicitly aware of from the more colloquial meaning of the term 'crusade', repackaging their legacy while keeping their name (Figure 1.1).

Nor were they alone in this. Twitter user Clare K, one of the numerous members of the public to engage with the debate, had tweeted at the time of the attack that 'if the Crusaders name was sourced from the Crusades then it would now be an important signal to condemn and rebuff the concept'.[55] Clare K was suggesting, seemingly, that it was indeed possible to say crusader and not mean a historical one: their 'if' gave the club the benefit of the doubt. For both the team and their public, it seemed, it was possible to say 'crusader' and yet somehow not be thinking of Christian war against the Muslims. The crusader iconography surrounding the Christchurch attack, then, concerned also the more general perception of the crusader movement among non-specialists of the era. If Tarrant picked carefully which elements of history he wanted to capitalise on, he was seemingly doing so against a much more fluid

Figure 1.1 Christchurch Crusader horsemen and fans ahead of the Investec Super Rugby match between the Christchurch Crusaders and Queensland Reds at AMI Stadium on 8 May 2015 in Christchurch, New Zealand. © dpa/Alamy Live News

background than we might expect, one on which it was seemingly considered possible to advertise a team through crusader re-enactors, and yet claim the idea of holy war was not necessarily implied by this.

Through the examinations of the propaganda of the Christchurch attack and reactions to it, then, we find a gap: that between plentifully available scholarship, in general agreement that Bohemond was not wholly invested in Christian war against Islam, and Tarrant's choice of him as a model for what he wanted to portray as a 'holy' battle; that between the historical associations of the word 'crusader', and those willing to leave the door open to uncoupling it from its origins. Tarrant's choice of Bohemond as a symbol for his Islamophobic terrorist act highlights how the task of the crusade historian in combating far-right use of crusader imagery lies in more complex terrain than we might immediately imagine, and restates the importance of engaging closely and attentively with the public and the uses to which the medieval past may be put. As Black classicist Dan-el Padilla Peralta has pointed out, it is not our role simply to 'point out the howlers', but to recognise and combat the risk inherent in the field itself, and the ways in which scholars must be alert to its potential for manipulation and appropriation.[56]

This chapter was born out of a desire to engage with something which I thought was my duty to address as a specialist in the field: the (to me) deeply surprising fact that a white supremacist terrorist should have used Bohemond – in scholarly analysis such an atypical representative of the crusader movement as 'holy war' – as a symbol for his propaganda. Throughout it, I have explored how separate the academic discourse is from the reality of the perception and use of this figure. In many ways, this chapter charts my own failure, that of recognising how the very history which I was studying fed into the larger appropriation of the medieval past. As Sierra Lomuto succinctly put it in her essay following the Christchurch attack: 'The historical accuracy of the referent isn't what matters: what matters are the conditions and contexts surrounding the referent in our own time'.[57] As Lomuto persuasively shows, merely 'reclaiming' the medieval past by correcting its misconceptions is not enough, as it continues not to address the way the concept of the medieval past in itself, and the use made of it by white agents specifically, may be liable to supporting them.

This chapter is, then, in many ways an acknowledgement of the ever-present difficulty in recognising how the history one specialises in is often received by the wider public, and radicalised agents within it, and indeed, to recognise that the complexity of academic debate, in and of itself, is a flawed instrument to tackle it. In the final instance, white academics such as myself may partake of the structural blindness which led me to be genuinely surprised when I discovered that the Christchurch shooter had identified in Bohemond an effective symbol for his own personal war against Muslim civilians, even as I should have realised why this could be. I began by saying that the use of Bohemond's name by Tarrant may have seemed 'an odd fit'; I conclude by pointing out that it should not have seemed so, had

I engaged more critically with the history I was looking at beyond the specialism of my own research. As Skottki puts it, 'the structural amnesia of historicism [...] obstructs our understanding of how such pasts might gain relevance again and resurface in unexpected coherences'.[58] Through the apparent incongruency of Bohemond's presence on the shooter's weapons, we see once more the difficulty in recognising the potential for threat inherent in contemporary memories of the crusader movement, and the scholar's duty to be alert for it and address it, challenging their own inherent perspective to do so.

Notes

1 My title references the important article by Luigi Russo, 'Bad Crusaders? The Normans of Southern Italy and the Crusading Movement in the Twelfth Century', *Anglo-Norman Studies*, 38 (2016), pp. 169–81. I am grateful to Charlotte Gauthier for her patience during the Covid-19 crisis and for all her work on this volume, to Jonathan Phillips and Mike Horswell for their useful suggestions at editing stage, to Hervin Fernández-Aceves for bringing to my attention Tarrant's use of the name of Bohemond, to William Alchorn for the discussion of ethical issues, to Benjamin O'Donnell for his help with the terminology of ammunitions, to Victoria Yuskaitis for helping access a few necessary materials, and to Andrew Hull and Goh Li Sian for their comments on a first draft of this chapter.

2 Hannah Ellis-Petersen, Graham Russell Kevin Ralinson, Elle Hunt, Matthew Weaver, Naaman Zhou, Kate Lyons, Christchurch shooting live blog account, *The Guardian*, 15–16 March 2019 <https://www.theguardian.com/world/live/2019/mar/15/christchurch-shooting-injuries-reported-as-police-respond-to-critical-incident-live>; Faisal Mahmud, 'New Zealand Mosque Attack: Who Were the Victims?', AL Jazeera, 22 March 2019 <https://www.aljazeera.com/news/2019/03/zealand-mosque-attacks-victims-190316183339297.html>; Emanuel Stoakes, 'New Zealand's Grief Turns to Joy as Mosque Shooter Brenton Tarrant Is Sentenced to Life in Prison', *The Washington Post*, 27 August 2020 <https://www.washingtonpost.com/world/asia_pacific/brenton-tarrant-sentence-life-prison-new-zealand-christchurch-mosque-shooting/2020/08/26/ddb9dc2a-e76a-11ea-bf44-0d31c85838a5_story.html>. All links in the chapter accessed June 2021.

3 Charles Anderson, 'Christchurch Shooting Suspect Will Face 50 Murder Charges, Say New Zealand Police', *The Guardian*, 4 April 2019 <https://www.theguardian.com/world/2019/apr/04/christchurch-shooting-suspect-will-face-50-charges-say-new-zealand-police>. I am indebted to the Sierra Lomuto essay 'Public Medievalism and the Rigor of Anti-Racist Critique', *In the Middle*, 4 April 2019 <https://www.inthemedievalmiddle.com/2019/04/public-medievalism-and-rigor-of-anti.html>, for highlighting the necessity of acknowledging and honouring the original Māori placenames.

4 Eleanor Ainge Roy and Charlotte Graham-McLay, 'Christchurch Gunman Pleads Guilty to New Zealand Mosque Attacks That Killed 51', *The Guardian*, 25 March 2020 <https://www.theguardian.com/world/2020/mar/26/christchurch-shooting-brenton-tarrant-pleads-guilty-to-new-zealand-mosque-attacks-that-killed-51>.

5 Alex Hern, 'Facebook and YouTube Defend Response to Christchurch Videos', *The Guardian*, 19 March 2019 <https://www.theguardian.com/world/2019/mar/19/facebook-and-youtube-defend-response-to-christchurch-videos>; Melissa Davey, 'Christchurch Shooting: Ardern Says "Manifesto" Sent to Office Minutes before Massacre', *The Guardian*, 17 March 2019 <https://www.

theguardian.com/world/2019/mar/17/christchurch-attack-death-toll-rises-to-50-as-concern-grows-over-burial-delays>.

6 Kevin Roose, ‘A Mass Murder of, and for, the Internet’, *The New York Times*, 15 March 2019 <https://www.nytimes.com/2019/03/15/technology/facebook-youtube-christchurch-shooting.html>; Taylor Lawrence, ‘The Shooter’s Manifesto Was Designed to Troll’, *The Atlantic*, 15 March 2019 <https://www.theatlantic.com/technology/archive/2019/03/the-shooters-manifesto-was-designed-to-troll/585058/>.

7 Chris Pleasance, ‘New Zealand Killer Scrawled “Inspiration” for His Shooting Spree on His Guns – from far-Right Murderers and Historical Figures to Sex Scandals Linked to Muslims’, *The Daily Mail Online*, 15 March 2019 <https://www.dailymail.co.uk/news/article-6812729/New-Zealand-killer-scrawled-inspiration-shooting-spree-guns.html>.

8 Ibrahim Al-Marashi, ‘The New Zealand Massacre and the Weaponisation of History’, *Al-Jazeera*, 24 March 2019 <https://www.aljazeera.com/opinions/2019/3/24/the-new-zealand-massacre-and-the-weaponisation-of-history>.

9 For ethical reasons, this chapter does not engage with the contents of Tarrant’s manifesto, and the author has not sought to obtain a copy, as the New Zealand government has banned its hosting and diffusion (Alexandra Mia, ‘New Zealand Made It Illegal for Anyone to Download or Share the Christchurch Shooter’s Manifesto’, *Business Insider*, 25 March 2019 <https://www.businessinsider.com/new-zealand-bans-christchurch-shooter-manifesto-livestream-2019-3?r=US&IR=T>). Ahmed S. Hashim, ‘Terrorism as an Instrument of Cultural Warfare: The Meaning of Anders Breivik’, *Counter Terrorist Trends and Analyses*, 3 (2011), pp. 1–6; Barry Richards, ‘What Drove Anders Breivik?’, *Contexts* 13 (2014), pp. 42–7.

10 Maev Kennedy, ‘Heather Heyer, Victim of Charlottesville Car Attack, Was Civil Rights Activist’, *The Guardian*, 14 August 2017 <https://www.theguardian.com/us-news/2017/aug/13/woman-killed-at-white-supremacist-rally-in-charlottesville-named>.

11 Josephine Livingstone, ‘Racism, Medievalism, and the White Supremacists of Charlottesville’, *The New Republic*, 15 August 2017 <https://newrepublic.com/article/144320/racism-medievalism-white-supremacists-charlottesville>.

12 Paul B. Sturtevant, ‘Leaving “Medieval” Charlottesville’, *The Public Medievalist*, 17 August 2017 <https://www.publicmedievalist.com/leaving-medieval-charlottesville/>; The Medieval Academy of America, ‘Medievalists Respond to Charlottesville’, *The Medieval Academy Blog*, 18 August 2017 <http://www.themedievalacademyblog.org/medievalists-respond-to-charlottesville/>; Dorothy Kim, ‘Teaching Medieval Studies in a Time of White Supremacy’, *In the Middle,* 28 August 2017 <http://www.inthemedievalmiddle.com/2017/08/teaching-medieval-studies-in-time-of.html>.

13 See, for instance, Cord J. Whitaker and Matthew Gabriele (eds.), ‘The Ghosts of the Nineteenth Century and the Future of Medieval Studies’, *postmedieval* 10.2 (2019); Ali Frauman, ‘Chasing Freyja: Rape, Immigration, and the Medieval in Alt-Right Discourse’, *Studies in Medievalism* 29 (2020), pp. 67–82; Louie Dean Valencia-García (ed.), *Far Right Revisionism and the End of History: Alt/Histories* (Abingdon, 2020); Mary Rambaran-Olm, M. Breann Leake and Micah James Goodrich (eds.), ‘Race, Revolt and Revolution’, *postmedieval* 11.4 (2020).

14 On the cultural and artistic relevance of Lepanto, see Víctor Mínguez, *Infierno y gloria en el mar: los Habsburgo y el imaginario artístico de Lepanto (1430–1700)* (Castelló de la Plana, 2018); James G. Harper, *The Turk and Islam in the Western Eye, 1450–1750* (Abingdon, 2016).

15 Charles Martel and the Battle of Tours (October 732) have long been a staple of far-right imagery, and their inclusion is unfortunately unsurprising, as discussed by

Daniel Wollenberg, 'The Battle of Tours and the US Southern Border', *Studies in Medievalism* 29 (2020), pp. 21–9.

16 Guardian Staff and Agencies, 'Canadian student pleads guilty to killing six men in mosque shooting', *The Guardian*, 28 March 2019 <https://www.theguardian.com/world/2018/mar/28/alexandre-bissonnette-canada-mosque-shooting-guilty-plea>; Guardian Staff and Agencies, 'Italian Extremist Given 12-Year Sentence for Gun Attack on Migrants', *The Guardian*, 3 October 2018 <https://www.theguardian.com/world/2018/oct/03/italian-extremist-given-12-year-sentence-after-shooting-at-migrants>.

17 Jasmin Mujanović (@JasminMuj), Twitter (X) thread, 15 March 2019 <https://twitter.com/JasminMuj/status/1106392602558062593>; Chris Arsenault, 'Why the Accused New Zealand Killer Was Fascinated with Serbia, Ottoman Empire', *CBC News*, 20 March 2019 <https://www.cbc.ca/news/world/new-zealand-mosque-massacre-bosnia-serbia-ottomans-1.5062886>.

18 Jason Wilson, 'Christchurch Shooter's Links to Austrian Far Right "More Extensive Than Thought"', *The Guardian*, 16 March 2019 <https://www.theguardian.com/world/2019/may/16/christchurch-shooters-links-to-austrian-far-right-more-extensive-than-thought>.

19 mg/is, 'Christchurch Attack: Polish Special Forces to Check "Polish Connections"', *Poland In*, 15 March 2020 <https://polandin.com/41765019/christchurch-attack-polish-special-forces-to-check-polish-connections>; Michael McGowan, 'Christchurch Suspect: Europe Investigates Possible Far Right Links', 18 March 2019 <https://www.theguardian.com/world/2019/mar/18/christchurch-suspect-europe-investigates-possible-far-right-links>.

20 'New Zealand PM slams book sales of Christchurch shooter's "manifesto"', *Dw.com*, 22 March 2018 <https://www.dw.com/en/new-zealand-pm-slams-book-sales-of-christchurch-shooters-manifesto/a-50119765>.

21 See, for example, Cecelia Holland, *Jerusalem* (New York, 1997); Jan Guillou, *Vägen till Jerusalem* (Stockhölm, 1998), first of a successful trilogy; Sharon Penman, *Lionheart* (London, 2011).

22 As stated above, I chose not to seek a copy of the manifesto. This reference was made, briefly, in a Tweet by security affairs analyst Divya Kumar Soti in a longer thread about Tarrant's references immediately after the attack (15 March 2019) <https://twitter.com/divyasoti/status/1106433255346065409>.

23 See Klaus Militzer, *Die Geschichte des Deutschen Ordens* (Stuttgart, 2012).

24 *Gesta Francorum*, ed. Rosalind Hill (Oxford, 1962), xxxviii, pp. 91–2.

25 *Albert of Aachen's History*, ed. and trans. Susan B. Edgington (Oxford, 2007), VI.29, p. 440; Guillaume de Tyr, *Chronique*, ed. R.B.C. Huygens (Turnhout, 1986); Ralph of Caen, *Tancredus*, ed. Edoardo d'Angelo (Turnhout, 2011).

26 William J. Purkis, Crusading Spirituality in the Holy Land and Iberia, c.1095–c.1187 (Woodbridge, 2008), p. 136; Simon Barton and Richard Fletcher, eds, The World of El Cid: Chronicles of the Spanish Reconquest (Manchester, 2001), p. 154.

27 Alejandro García-Sanjuán, 'Rejecting al-Andalus, Exalting the Reconquista: Historical Memory in Contemporary Spain', *Journal of Medieval Iberian Studies* 10 (2018), pp. 127–45.

28 Juan Diego Quesada and Fernando Peinado, 'How a Spanish Neo-Nazi became an International "Hero" of the Far Right', *El País in English*, 26 March 2019 <https://english.elpais.com/elpais/2019/03/25/inenglish/1553512492_825380.html>.

29 Kristin Skottki, 'The Dead, the Revived and the Recreated Pasts: "Structural Amnesia" in Representations of Crusade History', in *Perceptions of the Crusades from the Nineteenth to the Twenty-First Century: Engaging the Crusades, Volume One*, ed. Mike Horswell and Jonathan Phillips (London, 2018), pp. 107–32, 117, 118–20.

30 Jean Flori, *Bohèmond d'Antioche: Chevalier d'Aventure* (Paris, 2007); Luigi Russo, *Boemondo: Figlio del Guiscardo e principe di Antiochia* (Avellino, 2009), and Georgios Theotokis, *Bohemond I: Crusader and Conqueror* (Barnsley, 2021).
31 See Graham A. Loud, *The Age of Robert Guiscard: Southern Italy and the Norman Conquest* (New York, 2000).
32 Romuald of Salerno, *Chronicon*, ed. C.A. Garufi (Città di Castello, 1914), p. 200.
33 Jonathan Shepard, 'When Greek Meets Greek: Alexius Comnenus and Bohemond in 1097–8', *Byzantine and Modern Greek Studies* 12 (1988), pp. 185–277; Peter Frankopan, *The First Crusade: The Call from the East* (Cambridge, MA, 2012).
34 John France, 'The Use of the Anonymous *Gesta Francorum* in the Early Twelfth-Century Sources for the First Crusade', in *From Clermont to Jerusalem*, ed. Alan V. Murray (Turnhout, 1998), p. 30.
35 Russo, *Boemondo*, p. 165.
36 Thomas Asbridge, *The Creation of the Principality of Antioch (1098–1130)* (Woodbridge, 2000), pp. 53–60.
37 Alan V. Murray, 'The Enemy Within: Bohemond I and the Subversion of the First Crusade', in Crusading and Pilgrimage in the Norman World, ed. Kathryn Hurlock and Paul Oldfield (Woodbridge, 2015), pp. 31–48, 48; Vera von Falkenhausen, 'Boemondo I e Bisanzio' in 'Unde boat mundus quanti fuerit Boamundus', Boemondo I di Altavilla, un Normanno tra Occidente e Orient), ed. C.D. Fonseca e P. Ieva (Bari, 2015), pp. 105–23, 105.
38 Francesca Petrizzo, '"Most Excellent and Brave of Heart": The Making and Unmaking of Tancred in the Sources', in *The Making of Crusading Heroes and Villains: Engaging the Crusades, Volume Four*, ed. Mike Horswell and Kristin Skottki (Abingdon, 2020), pp. 7–24.
39 Steven Runciman, *A History of the Crusades: Volume II* (Cambridge, 1957), p. 51.
40 Alfred Duggan, *Count Bohemond* (London, 1964).
41 Laverne Gay, *Wine of Satan* (New York, 1949).
42 David C. Douglas, *The Norman Fate, 1100–1154*, (London, 1976), p. 181; Christopher Tyerman, *God's War: A New History of the Crusades* (London, 2006), pp. 110–12.
43 *Gesta Francorum*, xx, p. 44.
44 Douglas, *Norman Fate*, p. 181.
45 Guillaume de la Pouille, *La geste de Robert Guiscard*, ed., trans., comm. and intro. Marguerite Mathieu (Palermo, 1961), Book V; Orderic Vitalis, *The Ecclesiastical History*, ed. and trans. Marjorie Chibnall, 6 vols (Oxford, 1978), IV.32, pp. 164–8; Gaufredus Malaterra, *De rebus gestis Rogerii*, ed. Ernesto Pontieri (Bologna, 1927–28), IV.10, p. 91.
46 Annae Comnenae, *Alexias*, ed. Diether R. Reinsch and Athanasios Kambylis, Part I (Berlin, 2001), XIV.2, p. 332.
47 See Georgios Theotokis, *The Norman Campaigns in the Balkans, 1081–1108* AD (Woodbridge, 2014).
48 Goodreads user John Conquest summed up his takeaway as 'The Character Assassination of Alexios I Communions (sic) by the Coward Bohemond I', referencing the movie *The Assassination of Jesse James by the Coward Robert Ford* (2007), showing how effectively Frankopan's argument could be received by a non-academic reader, Goodreads, 1 November 2018 <https://www.goodreads.com/book/show/12907736-the-first-crusade>.
49 J. Stephen Roberts, Scott Amis and Andrew Buck, 'Bohemond, Antioch and the Crusades Podcast', *Real Crusades History*, 30 September 2015 <https://www.youtube.com/watch?v=ltwXoeLno5M&t=1s>; 'Bohemond I of Antioch', *Real Crusades History*, 13 February 2012 <https://www.youtube.com/watch?v=LDOtIs-2N-8>; 'Bohemond: Military Genius of the Middle Ages', 31 May 2013 <https://www.youtube.com/watch?v=hop_QTTBZp0>; '5 Epic Battles of Bohemond the Crusader', Real Crusades History, 2 February 2018 <https://www.youtube.com/watch?v=h2BPLH1UoYs>.

50 'Tancred, The First Crusade & The Rise of the Principality of Antioch (1096–1112)', *History Time*, 14 March 2019 <https://www.youtube.com/watch?v=aqsnNUlx1gc>; 'Bohemond of Taranto & the First Crusade', *History Time*, 20 May 2018 <https://www.youtube.com/watch?v=syB2Y5MF-aM>.
51 Adam M. Bishop, '#DeusVult', in *Whose Middle Ages? Teachable Moments for an Ill-Used Past*, ed. A. Albin et al. (New York, 2019), pp. 166–70.
52 'Christchurch shootings: Crusaders defend their name amid concerns it could be offensive', *Stuff*, 17 March 2019 <https://www.stuff.co.nz/sport/rugby/111334941/christchurch-shootings-is-it-time-the-crusaders-changed-their-name>; 'Crusaders rugby Team Retain Name Following Post-Mosque Attack Review', *BBC News*, 19 November 2019 <https://www.bbc.co.uk/news/world-asia-50596935>.
53 Matt McILraith, 'New Brand, Same Name but Crusaders Have Backing of Islamic Community', *The Guardian*, 1 February 2020 <https://www.theguardian.com/sport/2020/feb/02/new-brand-same-name-but-crusaders-have-backing-of-islamic-community>.
54 'Crusaders to Keep Name, Change Logo after Mosque Killings', *The Japan Times*, 29 November 2019 <https://www.japantimes.co.jp/sports/2019/11/29/rugby/crusaders-keep-name-change-logo-mosque-killings/#.XouzfFNKjoA>.
55 Twitter (X) user Clare K (@AucklandIsland), Twitter status, 16 March 2019 <https://twitter.com/AucklandIsland/status/1106732569356173312?ref_src=twsrc%5Etfw%7Ctwcamp%5Etweetembed%7Ctwterm%5E1106732569356173312&ref_url=https%3A%2F%2Fwww.stuff.co.nz%2Fsport%2Frugby%2F111334941%2Fchristchurch-shootings-is-it-time-the-crusaders-changed-their-name>.
56 Quoted in Rachel Poser, 'He Wants to Save Classics from Whiteness. Can the Field Survive?', *The New York Times Magazine*, 2 February 2021 <https://www.nytimes.com/2021/02/02/magazine/classics-greece-rome-whiteness.html>.
57 Lomuto, 'Public Medievalism'. This article was fundamental in showing me how I had been tackling this the wrong way, and the role my whiteness played in this.
58 Skottki, 'The Dead', p. 118.

Bibliography

Primary

Albert of Aachen's History, ed. and trans. Susan B. Edgington. Oxford: Clarendon Press, 2007.

Duggan, Alfred. *Count Bohemond*. London: Faber and Faber, 1964.

Gaufredus Malaterra. *De rebus gestis Rogerii*, ed. Ernesto Pontieri. Bologna: Zanichelli, 1927–28.

Gay, Laverne. *Wine of Satan*. New York: Charles Scribner's Sons, 1949.

Gesta Francorum et aliorum Hierosolimitanorum, ed. and trans. Rosalind Hill. Oxford: Clarendon Press, 1962.

Guillaume de la Pouille. *La geste de Robert Guiscard*, ed., trans., comm. and intro. Marguerite Mathieu. Palermo: Istituto Siciliano di Studi Bizantini e Neoellenici, 1961.

Guillaume de Tyr. *Chronique*, ed. R.B.C. Huygens. Two volumes. Turnhout: Brepols, 1986.

Guillou, Jan. *Vägen till Jerusalem*. Stockhölm: Norstedts Förlag, 1998.

Holland, Cecelia. *Jerusalem*. New York: Forge Books, 1997.

Orderic Vitalis. *The Ecclesiastical History*. Ed. and trans. Marjorie Chibnall. 6 Vols. Oxford: Clarendon Press, 1969–78.

Penman, Sharon. *Lionheart*. London: Macmillan, 2011.

Ralph of Caen. *Tancredus*, ed. Edoardo d'Angelo. Turnhout: Brepols, 2011.

Reinsch, Diether R. and Kambylis, Athanasios, eds. *Annae Comnenae Alexias*. Berlin: De Gruyter, 2001.
Romuald of Salerno. *Chronicon*, ed. Garufi. Città di Castello, 1914.

Secondary

Al-Marashi, Ibrahim. 'The New Zealand Massacre and the Weaponisation of History'. *Al-Jazeera*, 24 March 2019.
Asbridge, Thomas. *The Creation of the Principality of Antioch (1098–1130)*. Woodbridge: Boydell, 2000.
Barton, Simon and Fletcher, Richard, eds. *The World of El Cid: Chronicles of the Spanish Reconquest*. Manchester: Manchester University Press, 2001.
Bishop, Adam M. '#DeusVult'. In *Whose Middle Ages? Teachable Moments for an Ill-Used Past*, ed. Andrew Albin, Mary C. Erler, Thomas O'Donnell, Nicholas L. Paul and Nina Rowe. New York: Fordham University Press, 2019, pp. 166–70.
Douglas, David C. *The Norman Fate, 1100–1154*. London: Eyre & Spottiswoode, 1976.
France, John. 'The Use of the Anonymous *Gesta Francorum* in the Early Twelfth-Century Sources for the First Crusade'. In *From Clermont to Jerusalem*, ed. Alan V. Murray. Turnhout: Brepols, 1998, pp. 29–42.
Frankopan, Peter. *The First Crusade: The Call from the East*. Cambridge, MA: Harvard University Press, 2012.
Frauman, Ali. 'Chasing Freyja: Rape, Immigration, and the Medieval in Alt-Right Discourse'. *Studies in Medievalism* 29 (2020), pp. 67–82.
García-Sanjuán, Alejandro. 'Rejecting al-Andalus, Exalting the Reconquista: Historical Memory in Contemporary Spain'. *Journal of Medieval Iberian Studies* 10 (2018), pp. 127–45.
Harper, James G. *The Turk and Islam in the Western Eye, 1450–1750: Visual Imagery before Orientalism*. Abingdon: Routledge, 2016.
Hashim, Ahmed S. 'Terrorism as an Instrument of Cultural Warfare: The Meaning of Anders Breivik'. *Counter Terrorist Trends and Analyses* 3 (2011), pp. 1–6.
Kim, Dorothy. 'Teaching Medieval Studies in a Time of White Supremacy'. *In the Middle*, 28 August 2017.
Lomuto, Sierra. 'Public Medievalism and the Rigor of Anti-Racist Critique'. *In the Middle*, 4 April 2019.
Loud, Graham A. *The Age of Robert Guiscard: Southern Italy and the Norman Conquest*. New York: Longman, 2000.
The Medieval Academy of America. 'Medievalists Respond to Charlottesville'. *The Medieval Academy Blog*, 18 August 2017.
Militzer, Klaus. *Die Geschichte des Deutschen Ordens*. Stuttgart: Verlag W. Kohlhammer, 2012.
Mínguez, Víctor. *Infierno y gloria en el mar: los Habsburgo y el imaginario artístico de Lepanto (1430–1700)*. Castelló de la Plana: Universitat Jaume I, 2018.
Murray, Alan V. 'The Enemy Within: Bohemond I and the Subversion of the First Crusade'. In *Crusading and Pilgrimage in the Norman World*, ed. Kathryn Hurlock and Paul Oldfield. Woodbridge: Boydell, 2015, pp. 31–48.
Petrizzo, Francesca. '"Most Excellent and Brave of Heart": Tancred's Making and Unmaking in the Sources'. In *The Making of Crusading Heroes and Villains: Engaging*

the Crusades, Volume Four, ed. Mike Horswell and Kristin Skottki. Abingdon: Routledge, 2020, pp. 7–24.

Purkis, William J. *Crusading Spirituality in the Holy Land and Iberia, c.1095–c.1187*. Woodbridge: Boydell, 2008.

Rambaran-Olm, Mary, Leake, M. Breann and Goodrich, Micah James, eds. 'Race, Revolt and Revolution'. *postmedieval* 11 (2020).

Richards, Barry. 'What Drove Anders Breivik?' *Contexts* 13 (2014), pp. 42–47.

Runciman, Steven. *A History of the Crusades: Volume II*. Cambridge: Cambridge University Press, 1957.

Russo, Luigi. *Boemondo: Figlio del Guiscardo e principe di Antiochia*. Avellino: Sellino Editore, 2009.

Russo, Luigi. 'Bad Crusaders? The Normans of Southern Italy and the Crusading Movement in the Twelfth Century'. *Anglo-Norman Studies* 38 (2016), pp. 169–81.

Shepard, Jonathan. 'When Greek Meets Greek: Alexius Comnenus and Bohemond in 1097–8'. *Byzantine and Modern Greek Studies* 12 (1988), pp. 185–277.

Skottki, Kristin. 'The Dead, the Revived and the Recreated Pasts: "Structural Amnesia" in Representations of Crusade History'. In *Perceptions of the Crusades from the Nineteenth to the Twenty-First Century: Engaging the Crusades, Volume One*, ed. Mike Horswell and Jonathan Phillips. London: Routledge, 2018, pp. 107–32.

Sturtevant, Paul B. 'Leaving "Medieval" Charlottesville'. *The Public Medievalist*. 17 August 2017.

Theotokis, Georgios. *The Norman Campaigns in the Balkans, 1081–1108 AD*. Woodbridge: Boydell and Brewer, 2014.

Theotokis, Georgios. *Bohemond I: Crusader and Conqueror.* Barnsley: Pen and Sword, 2021.

Tyerman, Christopher. *God's War: A New History of the Crusades*. London: Penguin, 2006.

Valencia-García, Louie Dean, ed. *Far Right Revisionism and the End of History: Alt/Histories*. Abingdon: Routledge, 2020.

Von Falkenhausen, Vera. 'Boemondo I e Bisanzio'. In *"Unde boat mundus quanti fuerit Boamundus", Boemondo I di Altavilla, un Normanno tra Occidente e Oriente*, ed. C.D. Fonseca e P. Ieva. Bari: Società di Storia Patria per la Puglia, 2015, pp. 105–23.

Whitaker, Cord J., and Gabriele, Matthew, eds. 'The Ghosts of the Nineteenth Century and the Future of Medieval Studies'. *postmedieval* 10.2 (2019).

Wollenberg, Daniel. 'The Battle of Tours and the US Southern Border'. *Studies in Medievalism* 29 (2020), pp. 21–9.

News Articles

'Crusaders to Keep Name, Change Logo after Mosque Killings'. *The Japan Times*, 29 November 2019.

Ainge Roy, Eleanor and Graham-McLay, Charlotte. 'Christchurch Gunman Pleads Guilty to New Zealand Mosque Attacks That Killed 51'. *The Guardian*, 25 March 2020.

Anderson, Charles. 'Christchurch Shooting Suspect Will Face 50 Murder Charges, Say New Zealand Police'. *The Guardian*, 4 April 2019.

Arsenault, Chris. 'Why the Accused New Zealand Killer Was Fascinated with Serbia, Ottoman Empire'. *CBC News*, 20 March 2019.

BBC staff. 'Crusaders Rugby Team Retain Name Following Post-Mosque Attack Review'. *BBC News*, 19 November 2019.

Davey, Melissa. 'Christchurch Shooting: Ardern Says "Manifesto" Sent to Office Minutes before Massacre'. *The Guardian*, 17 March 2019.

'New Zealand PM Slams Book Sales of Christchurch Shooter's "Manifesto"'. *Dw.com*, 22 August 2018.

Ellis-Petersen, Hannah, Graham, Russell Kevin Ralinson, Hunt, Elle, Weaver, Matthew, Zhou, Naaman and Lyons, Kate, 'Christchurch Shooting Live Blog Account'. *The Guardian*, 15–16 March 2019.

Guardian Staff and Agencies. 'Italian Extremist Given 12-Year Sentence for Gun Attack on Migrants'. *The Guardian*, 3 October 2018.

Guardian Staff and Agencies. 'Canadian Student Pleads Guilty to Killing Six Men in Mosque Shooting'. *The Guardian*, 28 March 2019.

Hern, Alex. 'Facebook and YouTube Defend Response to Christchurch Videos'. *The Guardian*, 19 March 2019.

Kennedy, Maev. 'Heather Heyer, Victim of Charlottesville Car Attack, Was Civil Rights Activist'. *The Guardian*, 14 August 2017.

Lawrence, Taylor. 'The Shooter's Manifesto Was Designed to Troll'. *The Atlantic*, 15 March 2019.

Little, Becky. 'How Hate Groups Are Hijacking Medieval Symbols While Ignoring the Facts Behind Them'. *History.com*, 18 December 2017.

Livingstone, Josephine. 'Racism, Medievalism, and the White Supremacists of Charlottesville'. *The New Republic*, 15 August 2017.

Mahmud, Faisal. 'New Zealand Mosque Attack: Who Were the Victims?'. *Al Jazeera*, 22 March 2019.

McIlraith, Matt. 'New Brand, Same Name but Crusaders Have Backing of Islamic Community'. *The Guardian*, 1 February 2020.

McGowan, Michael. 'Christchurch Suspect: Europe Investigates Possible Far Right Links'. 18 March 2019.

mg/is. 'Christchurch Attack: Polish Special Forces to Check "Polish Connections"'. *Poland In*, 15 March 2020.

Mia, Alexandra. 'New Zealand Made It Illegal for Anyone to Download or Share the Christchurch Shooter's manifesto'. *Business Insider*, 25 March 2019.

Pleasance, Chris. 'New Zealand Killer Scrawled "Inspiration" for His Shooting Spree on His Guns – from Far-Right Murderers and Historical Figures to Sex Scandals Linked to Muslims'. *The Daily Mail Online*, 15 March 2019.

Poser, Rachel. 'He Wants to Save Classics from Whiteness. Can the Field Survive?'. *The New York Times Magazine*, 2 February 2021.

Quesada, Juan Diego and Peinado, Fernando. 'How a Spanish Neo-Nazi Became an International "Hero" of the Far Right'. *El País in English*, 26 March 2019.

Roose, Kevin. 'A Mass Murder of, and for, the Internet'. *The New York Times*, 15 March 2019.

Stoakes, Emanuel. 'New Zealand's Grief Turns to Joy as Mosque Shooter Brenton Tarrant Is Sentenced to Life in Prison'. *The Washington Post*, 27 August 2020.

Stuff staff. 'Christchurch Shootings: Crusaders Defend Their Name Amid Concerns It Could Be Offensive'. *Stuff*, 17 March 2019.

Wilson, Jason. 'Christchurch Shooter's Links to Austrian Far Right "More Extensive Than Thought"'. *The Guardian*, 16 May 2019.

2 Ordo Militaris Inc.

A Modern 'Military Order', Medieval History, and Historical 'Authenticity'

Rory MacLellan

Armed Christians led by a poor and chaste hermit, fighting against a supposedly expansionist and aggressive Islam. It sounds like an episode out of the First Crusade, but this contemporary group is actually a private military corporation based in Montana and the hermit a self-styled Franciscan from New Jersey. The Ordo Catholicus Militaris (OMC) was founded in summer 2016 and claims to follow in the footsteps of medieval military-religious orders like the Knights Templar, providing charity to their fellow Christians and fighting in their defence.[1] The OMC seeks to establish footholds across the world, provide humanitarian relief, and 'take up arms to defend fellow Christians when and where necessary [...] just as Blessed Urban II preached at Clermont 921 years ago'.[2]

The crusades, medieval knights, and the military orders have long held a fascination for the far-right. Mostly, such appropriations have resulted in little more than the adoption of the imagery or names of the military orders, but the OMC is among several far-right groups directly modelled upon the military orders.[3] Using the OMC's novel, as well as its radio programmes, social media, and recruitment brochure, this chapter first examines why the 'Ordo' and similar far-right groups are so attracted to the medieval period. It then argues that the OMC forgoes the pop culture references and memes so popular with other neo-crusaders and instead uses often obscure aspects of medieval history to create a sense of authenticity as a 'genuine' military order to recruit members and spread its ideology.[4]

At 39,000 words, the 'Ordo's' novel *On Becoming Soldiers of the Cross, Again!* is the most extensive example of the OMC's aims, beliefs, and infatuation with the medieval. Its author is Andrew J. Baalman, the Ordo's co-founder and radio host. The novel follows the adventures of seven Catholic American soldiers in Iraq fighting to defend Mosul against ISIS and the Iranian Revolutionary Guard. The author himself makes an appearance, in the guise of Sir Boleslaw, '1st cousin of 57 generations to Charlemagne'.[5] Disowned by their own country for fighting ISIS, the soldiers and Boleslaw become Polish citizens, with Boleslaw appointed the new king of Poland, instituting an ultra-nationalist reform of the country. With the help of the ghost

DOI: 10.4324/9781003033035-3

of Jan Sobieski III, electronic trebuchets, and a revived corps of Winged Hussars, the soldiers defeat the Jihadis. The reforms of Vatican II are overturned, Pope Francis and all of the 'evil' clergy are killed by a green spirit sent by God, and Pope Benedict XVI comes out of retirement to crown Boleslaw as ruler of the restored Holy Roman Empire.[6] The soldiers, mortally wounded in their final battle defending Mosul, spend their remaining days praying, building a monastery, marrying, and fathering children, before finally dying as martyrs.

The novel is immersed in a reverence for the medieval period and a desire to return to this supposedly simpler time. Its prologue is a two-part historical overview of how Europe has fallen from supposed unity in the medieval period into division and godlessness following the French Revolution. The first part, titled 'Who were the Christian soldiers?', presents a Catholic 'Golden Age' when all of Europe was unified under Catholic kings and militaries. If clergy were found to be committing crimes or preaching heresy, then they were removed from the priesthood and replaced by the pope. If a crusade or Holy League were called to defend Christendom, then all soldiers joined: 'On the most part, they loved Holy Mother Church, and protected Her from enemies within and without'.[7] This prologue's second part, 'How were the Christian soldiers turned into secular soldiers?', presents this unity as being destroyed by the 'secularists' behind the French Revolution. Baalman claims that it was at this time the 'Masonic' slogan of 'liberty, equality, fraternity' was born. According to the author, Bastille Day heralded the introduction of 'all modern problems', 'when Governments took God out of everything [...] including the proper training for soldiers'.[8]

The rest of the novel continues this theme, and even goes so far as to fetishise medieval weaponry. After discovering that they are descended from the original Knights Templar, the seven soldiers learn to fight with longbows, lances, and swords.[9] The soldiers leave for Iraq with their weapons, modern and medieval, including 'special Crusader Swords made out of Damascene steel; as the originals were'.[10] Upon arriving in Iraq, the soldiers use longbows to kill several snipers, as these are apparently more effective than modern weapons.[11] When defending Mosul, the soldiers build trebuchets with electric winches to increase the speed of reloading. Baalman writes that 'Our Blessed Lord tasked them to defend this city [...] using any and all means to do that; modern weapons and medieval weapons'.[12] The prose is intercut with several images of medieval events, figures, and saints, including the coronation of Charlemagne, Pope Urban II, Bernard of Clairvaux, St James Matamoros, a praying Templar, and the 1291 siege of Acre.[13] The soldiers experience visions of Bernard of Clairvaux and Urban II, and all are revealed to be descended from the original members of the Knights Templar.[14] When the soldiers father families, they name their children after medieval saints and rulers, including St Margaret of Scotland, Charlemagne, Gregory the Great, Richard I of England, Isabella of Spain, and Otto the Great, Holy Roman Emperor.[15]

Sir Boleslaw's accession as the king of Poland is followed by the new ruler restoring the 'ancient Catholic Constitution'. Boleslaw returns the Polish church to a state before the Vatican II reforms:

> The errors after Vatican II are banned. Sacred Music restored, Altar boys restored, Mass in Latin, the reception of the Eucharist on the tongue [...] Incense restored. IKEA tables removed, Mass on the Traditional Altars only [...] everything Catholic is restored!

Things perceived by the far-right as modern social ills are banned: abortion, contraception, same-sex marriage, euthanasia, and pornography.[16] All the 'liberal mayors' of Warsaw and other towns are removed and exiled, socialism is banned, Islam and the Quran are outlawed, the death penalty is restored for 'wicked crimes', and the country leaves the European Union. Thus, Boleslaw restores Poland to what the author sees as its ideal state: his interpretation of a society medieval in culture, politics, and religion. When the people of Europe then call for the return of their kings, God appears to Boleslaw, promising that 'Christendom will be restored', bringing Europe back to the idealised medieval period that Baalman presents in the novel's prologue.[17] This adoration of the medieval is shared by the OMC's other co-founder, Alexis Bugnolo, a Franciscan of private vows. In a 2016 interview, Bugnolo even went so far as to say of the Middle Ages that 'I wish it would come back'.[18] Medieval Europe was a 'beautiful society'.[19] He hopes that 'God willing, maybe the day will come' when a Catholic state establishes a 'crusading legion' in its armed forces.[20] For him, 'The whole spirit of our company is the crusades and what the crusaders did defending Christians'.[21]

The OMC's veneration for all things medieval is part of a long history of far-right medievalism. Members of the Ku Klux Klan of the early twentieth century could achieve several levels of 'knighthood' within the Klan.[22] Hiram Evans, Imperial Wizard of the Klan from 1922 to 1939, described the Klan as a successor to secret knightly orders of the 'Dark Ages'.[23] Heinrich Himmler incorporated Arthurian myth into his plans for the SS.[24] In 2004, members of the British National Party were told that their organisation was the only one fit to lead the 'New Crusade' needed to save Europe from the 'Islamic yoke'.[25] Six years later, the BNP's youth wing was renamed from the Young BNP to the BNP Crusaders in honour of those who had 'saved Christian Europe from the onslaught of Islam'.[26] Others on the far-right have, like the OMC, tried to emulate the military orders more directly, such as The Knights Templar International Novus Ordo Militiae (KTI). This British far-right organisation, founded by Jim Dowson, co-founder of Britain First, emerged in 2015.[27] New KTI members receive a cross pendant inscribed with the phrase 'militia templi', a flag of a red cross on a black and white field, modelled on the standard of the medieval Templars, and a copy of the KTI's 'Templar oath'.[28] The KTI even has an online 'armoury' selling replica medieval weapons and armour, including 'Lionheart swords' and 'Lionheart daggers' blessed by ordained priests.[29] All of these products are supposedly produced 'according to ancient traditions going back almost 1,000 years'.[30] This weaponry is marketed as a way to pledge allegiance to the group, its 'authenticity' tying the purchaser into a history (and supposed future) of defending Christendom:

> This incredible piece of History can be yours to hand down father to son until the call to arms comes again all across Christendom to rise and free our lands. (You may need Kevlar next time though, but still, the Templar Knight Helmet is a great Icon for all true Warriors).[31]

But what is it about the medieval period that is so attractive for the OMC and others on the far-right? For such groups, the crusades in particular hold such a strong appeal because they provide a history to look to in the face of the persecution of Christians or 'Islamisation' of Europe that these groups believe is happening, and an example of how to respond. They can present themselves as following in the footsteps of figures still widely venerated in popular perceptions of the Middle Ages, such as Richard the Lionheart or St Louis. With pop histories, films, and videogames of the crusades often portraying the military orders, particularly the Templars, as being the 'elite' of the crusaders, it is unsurprising that they have become the target of appropriation by neo-crusader organisations.[32] As to the medieval period in general, a false view of lost simplicity is attractive to these groups. *On Becoming*'s prologue claims that medieval Europe was unified under Catholicism, evil clergymen were easily removed from the priesthood, and Christendom was quick to unite in the face of outside aggression. The social reforms Sir Boleslaw undertakes in Poland all return the country to what Baalman sees as an ideal medieval state. Bugnolo claims that modern society has been 'demasculised' [sic] because men no longer learn archery, riding, or swordplay as they did in the medieval period (disregarding the fact that much of medieval Europe's population would have been too poor to own a sword or a horse).[33] Far-right forums such as *Stormfront* regularly host discussions about how the medieval period was actually one of 'great progress and light', when 'the white man was ENCOURAGED to research war, history, alchemy, literature, obedience, and leadership'.[34] The American Neo-Nazi *Renegade Tribune* sees the medieval period as 'an immensely creative time, a transition when the religious enslavement of our people was still uncertain [...] an Industrial Revolution'.[35] For the BNP, the medieval period and the crusades are a noble example of an earlier population responding to 'hundreds of years of savage and unprovoked relentless attacks' by rallying 'under the banner of the cross to defend themselves and fight back'.[36] The medieval period appeals to the far-right as a time when all the aspects of the modern world that they oppose were supposedly absent.

What distinguishes the 'Ordo' from others on the far-right is its preference to draw on aspects of medieval and early modern history, often obscure, over films, videogames, and memes. *Daily Stormer* articles attempt to explain the crusades through memes and try to promote medieval-set videogames that they believe align with their ideology.[37] The 'Defending the Crusades' page on Australian far-right site *Truthophobes* is also dominated by memes.[38] Brenton Tarrant, a far-right terrorist who massacred 51 people at two New Zealand mosques in 2019, encouraged others to 'even meme', to help spread far-right ideologies. 'Memes have done more for the ethnonationalist movement than any manifesto', he wrote.[39] The website *AltRight.com's* article on five steps to become a 'real man', is headed by an image of an armed and armoured Knight Templar from the film *Ironclad*.[40] The KTI's 'Templar oath' is an almost exact copy of the 'knight's oath' in the 2005 film *Kingdom of Heaven*.[41] Ironically, this is a film in which the Knights Templar are portrayed as villains and fanatics.

In contrast, the OMC rarely relies on memes or cinematic and videogame depictions of the medieval period. *On Becoming* references *Kingdom of Heaven* only twice in its 134 pages, the same number of times as it uses the phrase 'Kingdom of Heaven' in a religious context.[42] The only other instances of the OMC citing such films are in a couple of lone social media posts.[43] Bugnolo has even denounced *Kingdom of Heaven* as 'propaganda' and the 'bogeyman version' of the crusades.[44] The self-styled friar describes himself as a 'medievalist' who knows 'a lot about crusades, more than most people'.[45] Through his website, The Franciscan Archive, Bugnolo has published editions and translations of medieval theological texts, as well as his own theological writings.[46] He also founded The Scholasticum, a planned postgraduate institute for the study of medieval theology. Though he invited several academics to teach there, it appears to be a dead project.[47] Bugnolo's translations of medieval texts have even been cited by several academics.[48] His expertise in Latin and medieval theology allows the OMC to draw upon parts of medieval history either unknown or less accessible to the founders of most other neo-crusader groups.

The cover of *On Becoming* is not a still from a Hollywood film, but an illumination of three knights taken from a fourteenth-century devotional manuscript.[49] When the soldiers' chaplain, Father Hamel, visits Poland to ask for reinforcements to help defend Mosul from Jihadis, he visits the shrine of Our Lady of Czestochowa, an icon of the Virgin and Child of uncertain date and origin, appearing in Poland by the fourteenth century.[50] Whilst the icon is well-known in Poland, it is unlikely to be so familiar to the OMC's largely American audience. Likewise, the author notes that Jan Sobieksi arrives at Mosul accompanied by the same artillery commander he had at the siege of Vienna in 1683, Marcin Katski.[51] The final Jihadist attack on Mosul is defeated and the seven soldiers dealt their mortal wounds on the 6 May, which the text repeatedly notes is the feast of the 189 Swiss

Guards killed in the 1527 Sack of Rome.[52] That Baalman feels a need to explain the date's significance again and again suggests much of the OMC's audience may be less familiar with the more obscure aspects of history the 'Ordo' references. Sir Boleslaw's coronation as king of Poland is conducted using the Tridentine Mass, presented in the original Latin, followed in English by the coronation rite of the Roman Pontifical promulgated by Popes Benedict XIV (1740–58) and Leo XIII (1878–1903).[53] The sequence ends with 13 pages of the Latin Litany of the Saints.[54] None of the novel's illustrations are taken from pop culture; they are almost all historical artworks, sites, and artefacts, as well as maps and photographs of US troops and locations in Iraq.

The OMC's other outputs also draw upon less populist aspects of medieval history instead of the memes and pop culture portrayals of the period so favoured by others on the far-right. A nine-minute video promoting the 'Ordo' to investors begins with six minutes of manuscript illuminations, quotations from medieval figures, and photos of historic sites, attempting to draw a direct link between the medieval crusaders and the OMC.[55] Their radio show has included an episode on Catholic ethics in war, based on the fourteenth-century *De bello* by Giovanni da Legnano.[56] On 11 September 2019, and no doubt with the 9/11 attacks in mind, the OMC posted to Twitter (now 'X') a series of images quoting from speeches or papal bulls of Popes Urban II, Innocent III, and Eugenius III, all advocating war in defence of the faith.[57] The OMC's social media often highlights the feast days of somewhat obscure saints, such as Nicasius of Sicily and Gerard of Villamagna.[58] Both of these have even been adopted as the OMC's patron saints, alongside Charles the Good, count of Flanders, Matthew of Beauvais, Arnold of Hiltensweiler, Gospert of Aspremont, Louis IX of France, Bonifilius of Foligno, Francis of Assisi, Gilbert of Neufontaines, and Leonard of Reresby.[59] Again, except for Louis IX and Francis of Assisi, these figures are not nearly as recognisable or accessible as the memes and film stills used by other neo-crusader and far-right groups. Rather than due to any popular recognition, these figures were chosen because they all participated in a crusade, a point stressed in the OMC's biography of each of these figures. The use of sometimes obscure crusader saints, like Leonard of Reresby and Arnold of Hiltensweiler, adds to the sense of mystique and authenticity that the 'Ordo' aims to convey.

Such is the extent of the OMC's appropriation of medieval history that parts of the organisation's rule have even been adapted from that of the Knights Templar. The third clause of the 'Ordo's' rule begins:

> Let all you Catholics who renounce your own wills to serve the Sovereign King of the Universe, Christ Our Lord, for the salvation of your souls, for a fixed term, strive everywhere and always with pure desire to hear daily Mass.[60]

Compare with Judith Upton-Ward's translation of clause nine in the Templar's Latin Rule:

> You who renounce your own wills, and you others serving the sovereign king with horses and arms, for the salvation of your souls, for a fixed term, strive everywhere with pure desire to hear matins and the entire service.[61]

The fourth clause of the OMC's rule is also adapted from that of the Templars:

> If any secular soldier or any other man desires to leave behind the mass of perdition and abandon the life of worldliness and share Our company, let it not be consented that he be received immediately, as the Apostle St. Paul teaches, "Prove every spirit to see if it is of God".[62]

In clause eleven of the Templar Rule, this is rendered as:

> If any secular knight, or any other man, wishes to leave the mass of perdition and abandon that secular life and choose your communal life, do not consent to receive him immediately, for this said my lord St Paul: Probate spiritus si ex Deo sunt.[63]

To further drive home the connection, the OMC's rule is presented alongside an image of a manuscript copy of the Templar Rule.[64]

This medieval 'authenticity' is the OMC's unique selling point. Their recruitment brochure does not include a single meme or image from a film or TV series of the crusades. On the inside are images of a burning church, an ISIS fighter about to behead a captive in the street, and three burning corpses. On the reverse is the statue of Louis IX of France that stands in Aigues-Mortes, Camargue, where the king embarked for his first crusade in 1248. There is no caption in the brochure explaining who this statue depicts or the significance of its location as a crusade staging post. This unexplained image, also used on the OMC's homepage, combined with the brochure's claim that the OMC is 'a Military Order [...] a voluntary force to do the good after the example of the Holy Crusading Saints of old', is used to provide a sense of authenticity and authority, one reinforced by using references that their audience may not understand.[65] Bugnolo's presentation as a Franciscan friar, the use of parts of the Templar Rule and other Latin texts, even the OMC's Latin name, all combine to convey that this is not a group of amateurs who have watched *Kingdom of Heaven* one too many times, but an actual military order, a genuine modern crusade. As Bugnolo has said: 'the First Crusade was promoted by a hermit, so I can't see why [...] the crusade against ISIS can't be promoted by a hermit'.[66] But how effective is the OMC's preference for the obscure over the mainstream? The OMC claims to have several branches around the world, yet many of them appear to be dormant. The founder of their Portuguese chapter left the 'Ordo' in May 2018 and the Twitter accounts of the OMC's Polish, Portuguese, and Texan chapters have been inactive since 2018.[67] Their Spanish account is still active, but appears to be run by Baalman as it is largely concerned with retweeting his personal account.[68] The main OMC account has even admitted to an income of under $1,000 a year.[69] The OMC regularly announces new initiatives, often in response to recent disasters or conflicts, but there is little to show how effective these are.[70]

This message of supposed authenticity, a closer connection to the 'real' history of the crusades than that offered by other far-right and neo-crusader groups, is certainly distinctive to the OMC and an image it is keen to promote, even if it may lack popular appeal. Yet, the view of medieval history that the OMC conveys is often highly inaccurate. For Bugnolo, the true version of the crusades is that 'the crusaders were good and it was the Muslims who broke all the treaties and were out to kill and torment Christians for no purpose whatsoever'.[71] In fact, many treaties were broken by crusaders as well, such as Reynald of Chatillon's attack on a Muslim caravan in winter 1186–87 which helped end the truce between the Kingdom of Jerusalem and Saladin.[72] What is more, the range of factors behind the actions of the various Muslim states of the period can hardly be explained as merely random. The First Crusade's conquest of a large part of the Levant, including Jerusalem, a site holy to Islam as well as Christianity and Judaism, unsurprisingly led to further conflict. Bugnolo has also claimed that 'The Christian religion is probably the only one that has a concept of ethics in war', despite such a concept being well-evidenced in other religions such as Islam and even predating Christianity, stretching back at least as far as Ancient Egypt.[73]

The 'Ordo' has also promoted other, more specific errors. The St Nicasius that the OMC holds as a patron saint was probably fictional.[74] Bugnolo has described his 'Ordo' as being founded in the spirit of the 'crusaders of old who were all military orders of knights'.[75] In fact, only a fraction of those who fought in the crusades were members of military orders. For example, the contingent of Templar brethren, rather than troops raised by the Templars, at the Battle of Hattin in 1187 was probably no more than a few hundred men, as the order's grand commander described the 230 brethren slain there as a loss that had 'almost completely annihilated' the order's central convent.[76] In comparison, the entire Latin army at Hattin has been estimated at around 20,000.[77] What is more, the brethren of the military orders were not themselves crusaders, as they did not swear crusade vows. They were not even present in the First Crusade, which predated the militarisation of the Hospitallers and the foundation of the Templars.[78] As a fund-raising exercise, the 'Ordo' have begun selling one-gram palladium notes, one side depicting the crusader Raymond IV of Toulouse, the reverse showing a manuscript illumination which the 'Ordo' erroneously claims depicts Godfrey of

Bouillon fighting alongside Raymond of Toulouse in the siege of Tripoli.[79] Though Raymond and Godfrey, in the army of the First Crusade, did pass by Tripoli before conquering Jerusalem, Raymond's siege did not begin until 1102, three years after Godfrey's death.[80] The illumination is actually from a manuscript of the *Roman de Godefroy de Bouillon*, and does show Godfrey leading a siege, but the accompanying text makes no mention of Raymond or Tripoli.[81] Yet, the veneration of a fictional saint or the false description of a medieval illumination are not the sort of mistakes most of their audience will detect. The very inclusion of medieval manuscript illuminations and obscure saints in a group run by a self-professed medievalist and friar is enough to create this aura of authority and authenticity, regardless of whether that aura is justly earned. Those interested in joining a modern military order and becoming crusaders in the fight against Islamic terror likely already have the view that the crusades and the crusaders were noble and that the medieval period was a time when 'real' white, Christian men fought back against outside aggression.

This chapter has highlighted the existence of a relatively new far-right organisation and its extensive use of medieval history. The presentation of the OMC as a genuine military order founded by a Franciscan 'friar' and its emphasis on using medieval imagery and texts over memes and pop culture to create a sense of authenticity sets it apart from other neo-crusader groups on the far-right. Though, despite Bugnolo's claim to be a medievalist and someone who knows 'more than most people' about the crusades, his and Baalman's portrayal of the crusades and the wider medieval world is deeply inaccurate. Yet, these inaccuracies, whether about the character of the medieval period as a whole or the historicity of a single saint, matter little to the OMC's intended audience. If one is already attracted by the idea of becoming a modern-day crusader in a clash of civilisations between East and West, then one probably already has a rather simplistic view of the crusades. The more precise errors like the misdescription of a medieval illumination would go unnoticed except by those who had already studied the period at an advanced level.

The OMC has further plans to expand. Baalman has announced that he intends to release a further two books to promote the 'Ordo', the first 'reclaiming' the memory of the Templars from 'Masons' and 'secularists', the second an 'autobiography' of Hugh Capet of France, though both are yet to be published.[82] The OMC now offers a European youth camp programme and, since Russia's invasion of Ukraine in February 2022, has tried to attach itself to the Ukrainian cause via a new charity called Cross Azure, a reference to the OMC's blue cross logo.[83] With the ever-increasing appropriation of the medieval period by the far-right, the OMC's reliance on 'real' medieval history to win support may herald the start of a new trend on the far-right, with other neo-crusader groups also trying to promote a 'hidden true history' of the medieval world.

Notes

1 'The Justice of Our Cause', *Ordo Militaris Catholicus* <https://web.archive.org/web/20180220011332/https://www.ordo-militaris.us/2016/07/31/how-to-establish-the-order/> [accessed 28 August 2019].

2 'The Justice of Our Cause', *Ordo Militaris Catholicus*.

3 Rory MacLellan, 'Far-Right Appropriations of the Medieval Military Orders', *The Mediaeval Journal* 9 (2019), pp. 175–98.

4 Many of the sources cited here are webpages, and so are liable to be removed or modified in the future. Where possible, they have been cited here using archive.org's Wayback Machine, in order to preserve them for future study.

5 Andrew J. Baalman, *On Becoming Soldiers of the Cross, Again!* (Helena, MT, 2019), p. 48. Baalman has a great interest in researching his own ancestry, running a blog that proclaims his descent from seemingly every medieval Christian royal house: *Voice through My Ancestors* <http://myvoicethroughmyancestry.blogspot.com/> [accessed 25 February 2020]. *On Becoming*'s title page even declares the author to be a 'son of Charlemagne': Baalman, *On Becoming*, copyright page, title page.

6 Baalman, *On Becoming*, p. 127.

7 Baalman, *On Becoming*, p. 1. For wider Catholic uses of the Crusades, see Marco Giardini, 'The Reception of the Crusades in the Contemporary Catholic Church: 'Purification of Memory' or Medieval Nostalgia?', in *The Crusades in the Modern World: Engaging the Crusades, Volume Two*, ed. Mike Horswell and Akil N. Awan (Abingdon, 2020), pp. 75–90.

8 Baalman, *On Becoming*, p. 3. The Freemasons are a common far-right bogeyman and served as a bête noire for Nazi Germany, Vichy France, and Franco's Spain, as well as modern groups, though their inclusion in far-right invective today is more an inheritance from earlier traditions rather than representing a 'live issue': Michael Huysseune, 'Freemasonry/Freemasons, The', in *World Fascism: A Historical Encyclopedia*, ed. Cyprian P. Blamires and Paul Jackson, two volumes (Santa Barbara, CA, 2006), i, pp. 255–6.

9 Baalman, *On Becoming*, p. 24.

10 Baalman, *On Becoming*, p. 24.

11 Baalman, *On Becoming*, p. 26. Since the early modern period, the longbow has been a repeat subject of medievalism: Robert Hardy, *Longbow: A Social and Military History* (Yeovil, 1976), pp. 136–56.

12 Baalman, *On Becoming*, p. 50.

13 Baalman, *On Becoming*, pp. iii, 18, 20, 64, 98, 99.

14 Baalman, *On Becoming*, pp. 19–21, 24.

15 Baalman, *On Becoming*, pp. 116–17.

16 Baalman, *On Becoming*, pp. 93–4. Of course, each of these concepts, apart from legalised same-sex marriage, could be found in the medieval world as well: John M. Riddle, 'Oral Contraceptives and Early-Term Abortifacients during Classical Antiquity and the Middle Ages', *Past & Present* 132 (1991), pp. 3–32; Wolfgang P. Müller, *The Criminalization of Abortion in the West: Its Origins in Medieval Law* (London, 2012), pp. 162–70; Costas Tsiamis, Eleni Tounta and Effie Poulakou-Rebelakou, 'The "Endura" of The Cathars' Heresy: Medieval Concept of Ritual Euthanasia or Suicide?', *Journal of Religion and Health* 55 (2016), pp. 174–80; Martha Easton, '"Was It Good For You, Too?" Medieval Erotic Art and Its Audiences', *Different Visions: A Journal of New Perspectives on Medieval Art* 1 (2008), pp. 1–30.

17 *On Becoming*, p. 127.

18 'Brother Alexis Bugnolo ~ Ordo Militaris'.

19 Ordo Militaris Radio PR, 'The Vocation of the Christian Soldier in Ordo Militaris Inc', *Blog Talk Radio*, 2017 <https://web.archive.org/web/20170809101505/

https://www.blogtalkradio.com/ordo_militaris/2017/07/26/the-vocation-of-the-christian-soldier-in-ordo-militaris-inc> [accessed 14 October 2019].

20 Ordo Militaris Radio PR, 'The History and Reason for Ordo Militaris Inc', *Blog Talk Radio*, 2017 <https://web.archive.org/web/20191012172523/https://www.blogtalkradio.com/ordo_militaris/2017/06/29/the-history-and-reason-for-ordo-militaris-inc> [accessed 12 October 2019].

21 Ordo Militaris Radio PR, 'The History and Reason for Ordo Militaris Inc'.

22 Juan O. Sánchez, *Religion and the Ku Klux Klan: Biblical Appropriation in Their Literature and Songs* (Jefferson, NC, 2016), p. 45.

23 Sánchez, *Religion and the Ku Klux Klan*, pp. 46–7.

24 Martin Shichtman and Laurie A. Finke, 'Exegetical History: Nazis at the Round Table', *Postmedieval* 5 (2014), pp. 286–9.

25 Matthew J. Goodwin, *New British Fascism: Rise of the British National Party* (Abingdon, 2011), p. 164.

26 Goodwin, *New British Fascism*, p. 87.

27 Simon Cox and Anna Meisel, 'Is This Britain's Most Influential Far-Right Activist?', *BBC News*, 1 May 2018 <https://web.archive.org/web/20190710143752/https://www.bbc.co.uk/news/uk-43924702> [accessed 9 October 2019].

28 'Affiliate Membership', *Knights Templar International* <https://web.archive.org/web/20190330091147/https://www.knightstemplarorder.com/affiliate_membership> [accessed 9 October 2019]. For the medieval Templar flag, see *The Rule of the Templars: The French Text of the Rule of the Order of the Knights Templar*, ed. and trans. J.M. Upton-Ward (Woodbridge, 1992), no. 99.

29 'Templar Armoury', *Knights Templar International* <https://web.archive.org/web/20191011133842/https://www.knightstemplarorder.com/armoury> [accessed 11 October 2019]; 'Authentic Carbon Steel Templar Sword – Limited Stock!', *Knights Templar International* <https://web.archive.org/web/20190331024014/https://www.knightstemplarorder.com/templar-sword> [accessed 11 October 2019]; 'Lionheart Dagger', *Knights Templar International* <https://web.archive.org/web/20191011134115/https://www.knightstemplarorder.com/lionheart-dagger> [accessed 11 October 2019].

30 'Battle Axe', *Knights Templar International* <https://web.archive.org/web/20191011133718/https://www.knightstemplarorder.com/battle_axe> [accessed 11 October 2019].

31 'Battle Helmet', *Knights Templar International* <https://web.archive.org/web/20191011134209/https://www.knightstemplarorder.com/battle_helmet> [accessed 11 October 2019].

32 '[The Templars and Hospitallers] were fierce fighters who were feared far and wide in the Muslim world': Joseph Cummins, *History's Greatest Wars: The Epic Conflicts that Shaped the Modern World* (New York, 2013), p. 85. '[A] spiritualized version of modern-day elite military Special Forces': Karen Ralls, *The Knights Templar Encyclopedia* (Franklin Lakes, NJ, 2007), p. 105. 'a military elite group': Michael Haag, *The Templars: History and Myth* (London, 2008), p. 223. 'an elite military unit at the forefront of the crusader wars': Dan Jones, *The Templars* (London, 2017), p. 5.

33 'Brother Alexis Bugnolo ~ Ordo Militaris'.

34 'Top 10 Reasons the Dark Ages Were Not Dark', *Stormfront*, 4 December 2009 <https://web.archive.org/web/20180825215910/https://www.stormfront.org/forum/t662772/> [accessed 14 October 2019]; 'A Journey into the Middle Ages', *Stormfront*, 16 July 2014 <https://web.archive.org/web/20180913031142/https://www.stormfront.org/forum/t1052676/> [accessed 14 October 2019].

35 'The Middle Ages: Proud of Our Past', *Renegade Tribune*, 4 September 2016 <https://web.archive.org/web/20190328192327/http://www.renegadetribune.com/middle-ages-proud-past/> [accessed 14 October 2019].

36 Henry Watts, 'Rise of Christianity in England Attributed to Growing Patriotism', *British National Party*, 21 May 2017 <https://web.archive.org/web/20170824180015/https://bnp.org.uk/rise-christianity-england-attributed-growing-patriotism/> [accessed 14 October 2019].

37 'The Truth about the Crusades in Meme Form', *Daily Stormer*, 15 June 2014 <https://web.archive.org/web/20180809032404/https://dailystormer.name/the-truth-about-the-crusades-in-meme-form/> [accessed 11 October 2019]; Andrew Anglin, 'Trump Calls Putin after St. Petersburg Attack – Prime Alpha Males Agree to NEW CRUSADE!', *Daily Stormer*, 4 April 2017 <https://web.archive.org/web/20190909204354/https://dailystormer.name/trump-calls-putin-after-st-petersburg-attack-prime-alpha-males-agree-to-destroy-islam-together/> [accessed 11 October 2019]; Adrian Sol, 'New Non-Pozzed Game: Ancestor's Legacy', *Daily Stormer*, 2 June 2018 <https://web.archive.org/web/20190611035011/https://dailystormer.name/new-non-pozzed-game-ancestors-legacy/> [accessed 11 October 2019].

38 'Defending the Crusades', *Truthophobes* <https://web.archive.org/web/20191014141459/https://www.truthophobes.com/defending-the-crusades> [accessed 14 October 2019].

39 David D. Kirkpatrick, 'Massacre Suspect Traveled the World but Lived on the Internet', *The New York Times*, 15 March 2019 <https://web.archive.org/web/20191011112232/https://www.nytimes.com/2019/03/15/world/asia/new-zealand-shooting-brenton-tarrant.html> [accessed 25 February 2020].

40 Daniel Friberg, '5 Steps to Become a Real Man', *AltRight.com* <https://web.archive.org/web/20171019205022/https://altright.com/2017/09/30/5-steps-to-become-a-real-man/> [accessed 11 October 2019]; *Ironclad*, dir. Jonathan English (Warner Bros, 2011).

41 The KTI oath is: 'Be without fear in the face of your enemies. Be brave and upright that God may love you. Speak the truth, even if it leads to your death. Safeguard the helpless, and do no wrong': 'Affiliate Membership'. The film's version is: 'Be without fear in the face of your enemies. Be brave and upright that God may love thee. Speak the truth always, even if it leads to your death. Safeguard the helpless, and do no wrong': *Kingdom of Heaven*, dir. Ridley Scott (20th Century Fox, 2005). Stills of the film also feature on the KTI's website: 'History', *Knights Templar International* <https://web.archive.org/web/20190328105331/https://knightstemplarinternational.com/history/> [accessed 9 October 2019].

42 Baalman, *On Becoming*, pp. 50, 101, 115, 120.

43 A post using an edited image of James Purefoy as Thomas Marshall, the Knight Templar main character from the film *Ironclad*: Ordo Militaris Catholicus HQ, 'Christianity is essentially opposed to Freemasonry: Because the Christian seeks liberty from moral deviation and the Freemason seeks liberty from moral restraint the first has Christ as King the second a 3 headed Spider Demon!', *Twitter*, 26 February 2018 <https://web.archive.org/web/20190424000214/https:/twitter.com/MilitarisCath/status/968119426666192897> [accessed 10 October 2019]. A post with a still from *Kingdom of Heaven*: Ordo Militaris Catholicus HQ, 'Persecution of Christians will go on, so long as Christians tolerate being persecuted. However, if we but imitate the Crusaders of old, the persecution will come to a swift end! – True Christianity is not pacifism', *Twitter*, 25 June 2019 <https://web.archive.org/save/https://twitter.com/MilitarisCath/status/1143602750535688192> [accessed 10 October 2019].

44 Ordo Militaris Radio, 'The History and Reason for Ordo Militaris'.

45 'Brother Alexis Bugnolo ~ Ordo Militaris', *Youtube*, 7 December 2016 <https://web.archive.org/web/20191009123132/https://www.youtube.com/watch?v=MGtLGn6BvNM> [accessed 9 October 2019].

46 'FAQ', *The Franciscan Archive* <https://franciscan-archive.org/faq.html> [accessed 30 September 2019]; Francis of Assisi, *A Testament to Peace: the writings of St Francis of Assisi*, ed. Kajetan Esser, trans. Alexis Bugnolo (Mansfield, MA, 2008); Alexis Bugnolo, *30 Principles for the Scientific Study of Scripture* (Mansfield, MA, 2012); Alexis Bugnolo, *The Book of Tobias and Its Historical Narrative: A Historical-Scientific Study* (Mansfield, MA, 2012); St Bonaventure, *Commentaries on the First Book of Sentences of Master Peter Lombard Archbishop of Paris*, trans. Alexis Bugnolo (Mansfield, MA, 2014).

47 *Scholasticum* <https://www.studium-scholasticum.org/> [accessed 11 October 2019]; Jan Stevens, 'Deze kruisvaarders willen elke jihadist op aarde in de pan hakken', *De Morgen*, 21 May 2019 <https://www.demorgen.be/nieuws/deze-kruisvaarders-willen-elke-jihadist-op-aarde-in-de-pan-hakken~b8f09eed/> [accessed 11 October 2019].

48 For example: Philip C. Almond, *The Devil: A New Biography* (London, 2014), pp. 228–9, 236–7; Emmanuel Falque and Laure Solignac, 'Thinking in Franciscan: Part I', trans. Stephen E. Lewis, *Logos: A Journal of Catholic Thought and Literature* 21 (2018), pp. 56–9, nos 12, 15, 20, 23, 50, 53.

49 Baalamn, *On Becoming*, cover; Chantilly, Musée Condé, MS 167, f. 144r.

50 Baalman, *On Becoming*, p. 54; Robert Maniura, *Pilgrimage to Images in the Fifteenth Century: The Origins of the Cult of Our Lady of Częstochowa* (Woodbridge, 2004), p. 43.

51 Baalman, *On Becoming*, p. 60.

52 Baalman, *On Becoming*, pp. 97–8.

53 Baalman, *On Becoming*, pp. 72–5, 77–80. For the edition used by the author, see 'De benedictione et coronatione regis', *Liturgia Latina*, ed. David Forster <https://web.archive.org/web/20191010110146/http://www.liturgialatina.org/pontificale/120.htm?fbclid=IwAR1> [accessed 10 October 2019].

54 Baalman, *On Becoming*, pp. 80–92.

55 'Videos – Ordo Militaris Inc.', *Ordo Militaris Catholicus* <https://www.ordo-militaris.us/videos/> [accessed 25 February 2020].

56 Ordo Militaris Radio PR, 'Catholic Ethics in War', *Blog Talk Radio*, 2017 <https://web.archive.org/save/https://www.blogtalkradio.com/ordo_militaris/2017/09/08/catholic-ethics-in-war> [accessed 14 October 2019]; Giovanni da Legnano, *De bello, De Represaliis et De Duello*, ed. and trans. Thomas Erskine Holland (Oxford, 1917).

57 An image of Innocent III with a quotation from *Quia Maior* (1223): Ordo Militaris Inc., 'We are organised to do the Will of God! - Great is the merit and nobility of serving Christ the King! Join us! ordo-militaris.us', *Twitter*, 11 September 2019 <https://web.archive.org/web/20190927081236/https://twitter.com/Ordo_Militaris/status/1171804974495469568> [accessed 11 October 2019]. An image of Urban II with a quotation from Robert the Monk's record of his speech at Clermont: Ordo Militaris Inc., 'As Christians and members of the Church Militant upon Earth, it is the solemn duty and vocation of each of us to be Militant: all spiritually, and for some of us, actually, in the defense of the weak and innocent, who are persecuted! Do it with us http://ordo-militaris.us !', *Twitter*, 11 September 2019 <https://web.archive.org/web/20190927081413/https:/twitter.com/Ordo_Militaris/status/1171806154252541952> [accessed 11 October 2019]. Eugenius III and a quotation from Quantum Praedecessores: Ordo Militaris Inc., 'As Catholics we believe what Jesus said: "Give of what you have and it will be made clean for you", that is, that alms given in works of mercy obtain the remission of the punishments merited by sins. Be generous therefore http://ordo-militaris.us/donate to help persecuted Christians!', *Twitter*, 11 September 2019 <https://web.archive.org/web/20190913230550/https://twitter.com/Ordo_Militaris/status/1171806733376925697> [accessed 11 October 2019].

58 Ordo Militaris Catholicus HQ, 'PRAY FOR US! Blessed Gerard of Villamagna (1174–1242 A.D.), Italian Crusader, was Esquire to a knight. As a Crusader he was captured, later ransomed, then returned home. Franciscan tertiary (SFO). Lived the rest of his life as a hermit noted for his piety. May 13th Feast!', *Twitter*, 7 May 2019 <https://web.archive.org/web/20191011173619/https:/twitter.com/MilitarisCath/status/1125768703927209984> [accessed 11 October 2019]; Ordo Militaris Catholicus HQ, 'St Nicasius Camuto (1135–1187 A.D.) a Sicilian Member of the Knights Hospitallers & Crusader, fought in the defense of Acre. Captured by Saracens, who ordered him to renounce Christ; he refused & was beheaded. He is one of our primary Patrons. Feast Day: July 1st', *Twitter*, 12 June 2019 <https://web.archive.org/web/20191011174026/https:/twitter.com/MilitarisCath/status/1138801460383272963> [accessed 11 October 2019].

59 'Our Patron Saints', *Ordo Militaris Catholicus* <https://web.archive.org/web/20190330073011/https://www.ordo-militaris.us/our-patron-saints/> [accessed 11 October 2019].

60 'Our Holy Rule', *Ordo Militaris Catholicus* <https://web.archive.org/web/20190330174751/https://www.ordo-militaris.us/rule/> [accessed 10 October 2019].

61 *Rule of the Templars*, no. 9.

62 'Our Holy Rule'.

63 *Rule of the Templars*, no. 11.

64 The Templar Rule has also been appropriated by other groups, including Mexico's *Templarios* drug cartel: Phil James, '*Los Caballeros Templarios de Michoacán*: Knights Templar identity as a tool for legitimisation and internal discipline', in Horswell and Awan, *Crusades in the Modern World*, pp. 25–40.

65 'Ordo Militaris, Inc.'; *Ordo Militaris Catholicus: Defending Christians against the Terrors of our Age* (Helena, MT, undated).

66 'Mike Church Show: Brother Alexis Bugnolo - Ordo Militaris', *Youtube*, 6 October 2016 <https://web.archive.org/web/20191012145942/https://www.youtube.com/watch?v=nIcSEIvUy6o> [accessed 12 October 2019].

67 'It is sad to see our chapter founder for Portugal to go, but we will miss him and keep him in our prayers. So anyone in Portugal who are Faithful Catholics, Come To Join us at Ordo Militaris Catholicus! https://ordo-militaris.us', *Twitter*, 17 May 2018 <https://twitter.com/OrdoMilitarisPT/status/997236565062627328> [accessed 26 February 2020]; Katolicki Zakon Wojskowy - Kapituła Polska, *Twitter* <https://twitter.com/OrdoMilitarisRP> [accessed 26 February 2020]; Ordo Militaris Texas, *Twitter* <https://twitter.com/OMC_TX> [accessed 26 February 2020].

68 OMC Capitulo Nacional de España, *Twitter* <https://twitter.com/OrdoMilitarisES> [accessed 4 January 2024].

69 'Our PMC @Ordo_Militaris for example has donated over $9000 USD to persecuted Christians even though it has had a total income of less than $1000. We are a humanitarian organization and we live it sacrificially'. *Twitter*, 22 May 2019 <https://twitter.com/MilitarisCath/status/1131182011216015360> [accessed 26 February 2020].

70 'Help Ukraine! + Ordo Militaris', *Ordo Militaris Catholicus* <https://web.archive.org/web/20230529174734/www.ordo-militaris.us/help-ukraine/> [accessed 4 January 2024]; 'Armenian Refugee Fund + Ordo Militaris', *Ordo Militaris Catholicus* <https://web.archive.org/web/20240104161033/https://www.ordo-militaris.us/armenian-refugee-fund/> [accessed 4 January 2024].

71 Ordo Militaris Radio, 'The History and Reason for Ordo Militaris'.

72 Bernard Hamilton, *The Leper King and His Heirs: Baldwin IV and the Crusader Kingdom of Jerusalem* (Cambridge, 2000), pp. 225–7.

73 Ordo Militaris Radio, 'Catholic Ethics in War'; John Kelsay, *Arguing the Just War in Islam* (London, 2007); Rory Cox, 'Expanding the History of the Just War:

The Ethics of War in Ancient Egypt', *International Studies Quarterly* 61 (2017), pp. 371–84.

74 Jonathan Riley-Smith, *The Knights Hospitaller in the Levant, c. 1070–1309* (Basingstoke, 2012), p. 231.

75 Ordo Militaris Radio, 'The History and Reason for Ordo Militaris'.

76 Alan Forey, *The Military Orders: From the Twelfth to the Early Fourteenth Centuries* (Toronto, 1992), p. 79.

77 Jonathan Riley-Smith, *The Crusades: A History*, 2nd edn (London, 2005), p. 110.

78 Riley-Smith, *Knights Hospitaller in the Levant*, pp. 28–9.

79 'Palladium Notes', *Ordo Militaris Catholicus* <https://web.archive.org/web/20190706180110/https://www.ordo-militaris.us/palladium-notes/> [accessed 11 October 2019].

80 Simon John, *Godfrey of Bouillon: Duke of Lower Lotharingia, Ruler of Latin Jerusalem, c.1060–1100* (Abingdon, 2017), p. 158; Riley-Smith, *The Crusades*, p. 51.

81 Paris, Bibliothèque nationale de France, Fr 22495, f. 36r.

82 'Third New Book', *Ordo Militaris Radio*, 1 August 2019 <https://web.archive.org/web/20191015115334/https://ordomilitarisradio.wordpress.com/2019/08/01/third-new-book/?fbclid=IwAR2DJXdtgP-0v1h3aDZ0rgHJ_Cw5XgZ-_YRSCbFF00I3uprsMX7kuG-EbkA> [accessed 15 October 2019]; 'A Special Fourth Book for Ordo Militaris Catholicus', *Ordo Militaris Radio*, 4 August 2019 <https://web.archive.org/web/20191015115036/https://ordomilitarisradio.wordpress.com/2019/08/04/a-special-fourth-book-for-ordo-militaris-catholicus/?fbclid=IwAR06y3VeJFRP3RYf3sHHnH3Maaaw5CfHFgHyKfO9EZRBjHy-WP9kN-hE5Gcc> [accessed 15 October 2019].

83 'OMC Europe – Youth Camp + Ordo Militaris', *Ordo Militaris Cotholicus* <https://web.archive.org/web/20230924024323/https://www.ordo-militaris.us/join-ordo-militaris-catholicus-in-europe/> [accessed 4 January 2024]; 'Update on Alexis Bugnolo & Ordo Militaris', *Fr. Matthew P. Schneider, LC*, 7 June 2023 <https://web.archive.org/web/20230929160419/https://frmatthewlc.com/2023/06/update-on-alexis-bugnolo-ordo-militaris/> [accessed 4 January 2024].

Bibliography

Archival

Chantilly, Musée Condé, MS 167.

Paris, Bibliothèque nationale de France, Fr 22495.

Primary

Baalman, Andrew J. *On Becoming Soldiers of the Cross, Again!* Helena, MT: Ordo Militaris, 2019.

St Bonaventure. *Commentaries on the First Book of Sentences of Master Peter Lombard Archbishop of Paris*, trans. Alexis Bugnolo. Mansfield, MA: Franciscan Archive, 2014.

Francis of Assisi. *A Testament to Peace: The Writings of St Francis of Assisi*, ed. Kajetan Esser, trans. Alexis Bugnolo. Mansfield, MA: Franciscan Archive, 2008.

Giovanni da Legnano. *De bello, De Represaliis et De Duello*, ed. and trans. Thomas Erskine Holland. Oxford: Oxford University Press, 1917.

Ironclad. Dir. Jonathan English. Warner Bros, 2011.

Kingdom of Heaven. Dir. Ridley Scott. 20th Century Fox, 2005.
Ordo Militaris Catholicus: Defending Christians against the Terrors of our Age. Helena, MT: Ordo Militaris, undated.
Upton-Ward, J.M., ed. and trans. *The Rule of the Templars: The French Text of the Rule of the Order of the Knights Templar*. Woodbridge: Boydell, 1992.

Secondary

Almond, Philip C. *The Devil: A New Biography*. London: I.B. Tauris, 2014.
Blamires, Cyprian P. and Jackson, Paul, eds. *World Fascism: A Historical Encyclopedia*. Two volumes. Santa Barbara, CA: ABC-CLIO, 2006.
Bugnolo, Alexis. *30 Principles for the Scientific Study of Scripture*. Mansfield, MA, 2012.
Bugnolo, Alexis. *The Book of Tobias and its Historical Narrative: A Historical-Scientific Study*. Mansfield, MA, 2012.
Cox, Rory. 'Expanding the History of the Just War: The Ethics of War in Ancient Egypt'. *International Studies Quarterly* 61 (2017), pp. 371–84.
Cummins, Joseph. *History's Greatest Wars: The Epic Conflicts that Shaped the Modern World*. New York: Crestline, 2013.
Dillard, Peter S. *A Way into Scholasticism: A Companion to St. Bonaventure's The Soul's Journey into God*. Cambridge: James Clarke, 2012.
Easton, Martha. '"Was It Good for You, Too?" Medieval Erotic Art and Its Audiences'. *Different Visions: A Journal of New Perspectives on Medieval Art* 1 (2008), pp. 1–30.
Falque, Emmanuel and Solignac, Laure. 'Thinking in Franciscan: Part I', trans. Stephen E. Lewis. *Logos: A Journal of Catholic Thought and Literature* 21 (2018), pp. 31–59.
Forey, Alan. *The Military Orders: From the Twelfth to the Early Fourteenth Centuries*. Toronto: University of Toronto Press, 1992.
Goodwin, Matthew J. *New British Fascism: Rise of the British National Party*. Abingdon: Routledge, 2011.
Haag, Michael. *The Templars: History and Myth*. London: Profile Books, 2008.
Hamilton, Bernard. *The Leper King and His Heirs: Baldwin IV and the Crusader Kingdom of Jerusalem*. Cambridge: Cambridge University Press, 2000.
Hardy, Robert. *Longbow: A Social and Military History*. Yeovil: Haynes, 1976.
Horswell, Mike and Awan, Akil N., eds. *The Crusades in the Modern World*, Engaging the Crusades, 2. Abingdon: Routledge, 2020.
John, Simon. *Godfrey of Bouillon: Duke of Lower Lotharingia, Ruler of Latin Jerusalem, c.1060–1100*. Abingdon: Routledge, 2017.
Jones, Dan. *The Templars*. London: Head of Zeus, 2017.
Kelsay, John. *Arguing the Just War in Islam*. London: Harvard University Press, 2007.
MacLellan, Rory. 'Far-Right Appropriations of the Medieval Military Orders'. *The Mediaeval Journal* 9 (2019), pp. 175–98.
Maniura, Robert. *Pilgrimage to Images in the Fifteenth Century: The Origins of the Cult of Our Lady of Częstochowa*. Woodbridge: Boydell, 2004.
Merchant, Carolyn. *Autonomous Nature: Problems of Prediction and Control from Ancient Times to the Scientific Revolution*. Abingdon: Routledge, 2016.
Morgan, Ruth A. and Smith, James L. 'Premodern Streams of Thought in Twenty-First-Century Water Management'. *Radical History Review* 116 (2013), pp. 105–29.

Müller, Wolfgang P. *The Criminalization of Abortion in the West: Its Origins in Medieval Law*. London: Cornell University Press, 2012.

Ralls, Karen. *The Knights Templar Encyclopedia*. Franklin Lakes, NJ: New Page, 2007.

Raymond, Joad. *Milton's Angels: The Early-Modern Imagination*. Oxford: Oxford University Press, 2010.

Riddle, John M. 'Oral Contraceptives and Early-Term Abortifacients during Classical Antiquity and the Middle Ages'. *Past & Present* 132 (1991), pp. 3–32.

Riley-Smith, Jonathan. *The Crusades: A History*. 2nd edn. London: Yale, 2005.

Riley-Smith, Jonathan. *The Knights Hospitaller in the Levant, c. 1070–1309*. Basingstoke: Palgrave, 2012.

Sánchez, Juan O. *Religion and the Ku Klux Klan: Biblical Appropriation in Their Literature and Songs*. Jefferson, NC: McFarland, 2016.

Shichtman, Martin and Finke, Laurie A. 'Exegetical History: Nazis at the Round Table'. *Postmedieval* 5 (2014), pp. 278–94.

Tsiamis, Costa, Tounta, Eleni and Poulakou-Rebelakou, Effie. 'The "Endura" of the Cathars' Heresy: Medieval Concept of Ritual Euthanasia or Suicide?' *Journal of Religion and Health* 55 (2016), pp. 174–80.

Selected Websites

AltRight.com. https://altright.com/ (accessible through archive.org's Wayback Machine).

Blog Talk Radio. www.blogtalkradio.com/.

British National Party. bnp.org.uk/.

Daily Stormer. https://dailystormer.name/.

De Morgen. www.demorgen.be/.

The Franciscan Archive. https://franciscan-archive.org/.

Knights Templar International. https://knightstemplarinternational.com/.

Liturgia Latina. www.liturgialatina.org/.

Ordo Militaris Catholicus. https://ordo-militaris.us/.

Ordo Militaris Radio. https://ordomilitarisradio.wordpress.com/.

Renegade Tribune. www.renegadetribune.com/.

The Scholasticum. https://www.studium-scholasticum.org/.

Stormfront. www.stormfront.org/.

Truthophobes. www.truthophobes.com/ (accessible through archive.org's Wayback Machine).

Voice Through My Ancestors. http://myvoicethroughmyancestry.blogspot.com/.

3 British Newspapers, Brexit, and the Little Crusaders of Middle England

Andrew B.R. Elliott

On 8 January 2011, the British populist right-wing tabloid *The Daily Express* launched a special edition of their newspaper to mark their campaign to leave the EU. Along with a 'pull out and keep' souvenir version of the poster, the paper featured a curious front-page image of a cartoon of a red-and-white knight, standing defiantly – if rather implausibly, given the scale of the drawing – on the edge of the cliffs of Dover. He holds a spear in his right hand, pointing vaguely out to sea, and in his left is a shield on which is drawn a red cross on a white background, with a downward-facing sword. A large speech bubble next to the chainmail-clad knight announces that 'we <u>demand</u> our country back!' The headline reads: 'GET BRITAIN OUT OF THE EU' (Figure 3.1).

There are two important facets to this rather garish front cover. First, it backdates the power, tenor, and tenacity of the Brexit discourse to at least five years before the actual referendum which took place in 2016. Relying on the common association between knights and crusades, the *Express* openly linked its masthead knight to the campaign, pledging that from that day forward, their crusader masthead would stand for their attempt to leave the European Union by calling for a referendum on the subject. As the article claims, 'the famous and symbolic Crusader who adorns our masthead will become the figurehead of the struggle to repatriate British sovereignty from a political project that has comprehensively failed people right across Europe'.[1]

The 2011 cover thus drew on a feeling of popular support which the *Express* had managed to cultivate among its readership and – more deeply than that – a sense of what a crusader might represent to such an audience. An earlier 2010 launch issue had printed 'coupons' which they encouraged their readers to use as a means to express opposition to the EU. By the end of that year, some 300,000 coupons had been dutifully posted to local MPs and the *Express* head office, representing a surprising (to Remainers, at least) testament to the strength of anti-EU feeling already existing among Middle England. Indeed, for those outside the UK who might be rather baffled by the apparently sudden emergence of anti-European discourse, knowing the backstory offers greater clarity about the growing unease on which UKIP had

DOI: 10.4324/9781003033035-4

Figure 3.1 Leave supporter in Blackpool wearing hi-vis jacket emblazoned with the Daily Express 'Get Britain Out of the EU' cover, 25 June 2016. © Media-WorldImages/Alamy Live News

been capitalising already for a decade. It also helps to explain why in 2013 the somewhat beleaguered (but coalition-backed) Prime Minister, David Cameron, would concede to the request for a referendum in the first place. Far from a sudden turn, in reality, the story had been brewing for long enough that by 2011 the *Express* were confident enough that they had the backing of the right-wing readership to devote their front cover to the movement.

The second facet of that cover concerns its semiotic power. A closer reading of the image shows how pernicious that rhetoric was, and to what extent the crusades, and the memory of them, 'continue to haunt our contemporary collective memory'.[2] It is clear that these political medievalisms are deeply rooted within a debate which extends far beyond a simple reference to the medieval past, but rather ties in with a broader restlessness rooted in both a myth of nations and, as I will show later, an imagined community.

Though, of course, the 2011 Special Edition was not the first instance of such anti-European sentiment from the conservative right wing, the campaign would have a long-lasting impact in the fraught negotiations surrounding the future of Britain's relationship with the EU. What is particularly interesting throughout the ensuing furore, however, is not only the brazen nationalist politics, but the instant recourse to a series of medievalisms as part of both sides of the campaign: in particular, the image of a crusading knight, and the choice to call the campaign a crusade, though there are several other medievalisms which will be discussed below.

Indeed, while it is a curious front cover even by the *Express*'s standards, the sentiments it conveys are in fact typical of the Brexit discourse, and this kind of image would become characteristic of the Brexit debate.[3] It is unambiguous, immediately comprehensible, and relies on the recognition of a series of elements coded as part of a project of national belonging.[4] If one looks more closely at the cliffs, it is clear that there are some stylised birds flying over the top of them and in the background. What might surprise readers outside of or unfamiliar with the UK, is that these birds do not need to be recognisable graphically to play a powerfully nostalgic role in the minds of the *Express* readership. To many British readers of a specific generation, they are instantly identified as bluebirds, indexically referring to a Vera Lynn song from the Second World War, 'We'll meet again', which contains the famous opening line, 'there'll be bluebirds over the White Cliffs of Dover'.

The fact that bluebirds are not indigenous to the UK is inconsequential: the connotative image belongs the realm of national myth and a pervasive nationalist nostalgia, recalling an entirely invented idea of Britain as a colonial superpower, a driving factor in the triumphalist rhetoric of Brexitese. Thus, all three symbols (knight, cliffs, birds) combine to offer a dizzying cocktail of jumbled memories from O-Level history classes whose potency is sufficient to render a tranche of Middle England weak at the knees, recalling the legend of Cnut shouting at waves, a misremembered repulsion of the Vikings in 1066, the somewhat ironic celebration of the Norman Conquest in the same year, through to the Spanish Armada of 1588, and the Battle of Britain in 1940 in which aerial warfare took place within sight of the cliffs, even if these moments have become more mythological than historical.

The intervening years, of course, saw a great deal of friction, division, and outright hostility between the pro- and anti-European factions which arose (dubbed Remain and Leave, respectively), which was scarcely resolved by the UK's marginal (52% of the 72.2% turnout) majority to leave the EU after the 2016 referendum, a movement referred to by the portmanteau Brexit. Having tied its colours to the mast without ambiguity, the *Express*'s crusader played a provocative role in the debacle, and in particular by insisting upon a clearly identifiable 'us and them' dynamic throughout.

The Little Crusader and the Defence of Little Britain

The Little Crusader's symbolic value activates two temporal planes simultaneously, even if one of those planes is entirely fictitious. As a medieval crusader, it is an entirely ahistorical (one newspaper talks about an 'Anglo-Saxon crusade')[5] and invented tradition which fulfils what Patrick Geary describes as a 'Myth of Nations', and what Hobsbawm describes as an invented tradition.[6]

As well as a mythical protector of Great Britain, the mascot also serves as the identifiable symbol of *The Express* newspaper itself. The so-called 'Little Crusader' has had a long association with the newspaper, appearing on its masthead since 1929 when its owner Lord Beaverbrook introduced it as part of his own 'Imperial Crusade'. According to Tim de Lisle:

> When Beaverbrook, then Mr Max Aitken, bought the paper in 1916, the only symbol next to the title was the royal coat of arms. So it remained until 1929, when Beaverbrook launched a campaign for free trade within the British Empire. On 11 July 1929 Beaverbrook wrote the Express's splash (front-page lead item) himself. '*I have combined with the Daily Express*', he declared, '*to launch the Imperial Crusade*'. His motive was partly a wish to protect his native Canada from being annexed, in trade terms, by the United States, and partly to push Stanley Baldwin out of the Tory leadership. The symbol followed shortly afterwards. It looked exactly as it does today: a crusader, in profile, wearing chainmail and helmet, sword drawn, shield in place and showing a dagger superimposed on a cross. Beaverbrook's crusade was more than just a newspaper campaign. It had its own office, staff, a steering committee drawn from the great and the good (paid, furtively, by Beaverbrook), and candidates in by-elections.[7]

The crusade was abandoned in 1931 through lack of support, but the little crusader in the masthead would live on, as would the editorials linking the mascot to the political tenor of the issues of the day. Already nostalgicised, tellingly the crusader was perceived by Beaverbrook as 'a memorial to a lost campaign', and would become more emphatically so through its reuse over the years.

Having adorned the paper for 22 years as a symbol of the failing Empire Crusade, in 1953 the mascot's postwar symbolism suddenly ramped up when it became tied again to a different waning Empire. The second phase of its politicisation came again on an economic front, with resistance to the nascent Common Market.

> [The] free traders were in the ascendant and his [Beaverbrook's] protectionist and imperialist views were scorned. In an act of spite or frustration,

> or both, Beaverbrook ordered the crusader symbol, which had appeared on the paper's masthead since the 1931 launch of his Empire Crusade, to be chained. Most *Daily Express* readers, if they noticed at all, were probably baffled.[8]

In this move, it is possible to read Beaverbrook's nostalgic fetishisation of a British imperialism; the depiction of the crusader in chains in 1951 thus came to denote the demise of the British Empire (and British imperial power) a concept which became a topos of the newspaper's right-wing politics.

When Britain was invited to join the Common Market (which would later become the EU) in 1961, the chained crusader was revived once again, with Beaverbrook declaring that he would be removed from his chains 'the day the Common Market is beaten'.[9] It is unclear precisely when they were removed, but it seems that they were quietly retired soon afterwards.[10] Indeed even without the chained crusader, by the following year *The Express* had already returned to its favourite theme of sovereignty, once again invoking the invented traditions of the Middle Ages as a founding period of British history. The coverage overtly conjured up a sense of British exceptionalism in Anglo-European relations, claiming a confused combination of 'Magna Carta, Trafalgar and the Reform Bill as testaments to British independence [*Daily Express*, 30 March 1962] while the *Sunday Express* invoked the Armada, Napoleon and World War II'.[11]

Clearly, then, the newspaper's masthead crusader repeatedly conflates the crusader with empire and commonwealth, which all end up overlapping into a confused maelstrom of postcolonial nostalgia. The little crusader begins life being explicitly linked to the commonwealth, by which Beaverbrook and his editing team intended to signal white-majority nations, including Canada, Australia, New Zealand, and parts of South Africa. In the face of failure, the newspaper's crusader is shifted to symbolise opposition to Common Market – once again dredging up the empire in its 'Commonwealth not Common Market' slogan which summarised this post-Second World War position. Then, with the coming of the EEC, their resistance to this exclusion of global community in favour of a European one manifests itself once again in the crusader-in-chains analogy not only as a symbol of Britain being 'curtailed', but as a nod to the late Beaverbrook (he died in 1964) and his crusading legend.

> As both symbolic device and barometer of literal intent, Beaverbrook's chained icon affords convenient access to the world-view of the *Daily Express*. Spiritually, the Crusader manifested an ethos of moralistic dissent and a quest through battle for honour, if not immortality. Moreover, as the public knew, the Crusader's implied meanings accorded with the character and aspirations of its owner.[12]

'The Crusader' is also, as it happens, the name given to the *Express*'s advice column, devoted to bringing justice to the various plights of its readers. While the Crusader's campaigns sometimes redress genuine injustices, just as often their crusades are significantly less profound, reflecting the minor quibbles of entitled, and mildly disgruntled, consumers. For instance, the 27 January 2020 column took up arms against insufficient compensation for an error in the braking system for a VW Tiguan on 27 January 2020. On 25 February 2019, it waged war on behalf of a magazine subscriber who did not receive their full annual subscription. The 3 February 2020 column bemoaned a faulty direct debit on an electricity bill for an owner's holiday home in Devon, meaning that their beach hut was slightly overcharged. In the 8 April 2019 edition, the Crusader recounted the woes of a couple who felt aggrieved that the sale fell through for a second home they'd bought as an investment. The couple had seemingly contacted the column to recover the £500 reservation fee and to seek compensation for lost interest on the £150,000 cash which they had to hold in their current account (instead of their savings) in order to proceed with the mortgage-free purchase of their investment property.

While of course, it is tempting to poke fun at the particular brand of entitlement which haunts the pages of the column, that is not my point. Rather, it is intriguing to contrast the banality of these consumer complaints with the gravity of a deeply charged term like 'crusader'. Irrespective of the intention lying behind the word, what is happening with the *Express*'s Little Crusader is a transition from one set of symbolic indices to a symbol (in the truly Peircean sense of those terms).[13] The fact that the term has been sufficiently banalised to describe a fight against a faceless corporation is important. Despite being deployed in different contexts, the Little Crusader quickly became synonymous not only with the paper, but with the ethics and substance of its various crusades. So regular and mundane are they that the knight is parodied in the satirical current affairs magazine *Private Eye*, whose masthead prominently features a knight called 'Gnitty', who brandishes a comically bent sword, with seemingly Freudian connotations.

Nevertheless, banal and unremarkable as they might appear, it is clear that the term 'Crusader' is not meaningless. In all of the examples explored for this chapter, there are three common traits which recur throughout:

1 it is a battle fought on behalf of the (ostensibly) vulnerable
2 it is a battle fought against a faceless and obfuscatory enemy
3 it is a battle fought on ideological lines which are obscured in order to pretend that a given political stance is the norm. In those cases above, each war is waged in the name of a self-proclaimed 'common sense', on behalf of a 'morally-upright taxpayer'.

Consequently, on closer analysis, it is obvious that there is something deeply meaningful about the use of a term like 'crusader' here. It is not that the idea of a crusader is neutralised as a banal medievalism (though it can be). The fact that it also finds itself resurrected periodically in the service of a political crusade means that it has *not been neutralised* at all.

The term is, in reality, still just as politically charged as it ever was, but more insidious in the ways in which it has been politicised through repetition, drawing in issues of relational and situational meaning, rather than any absolute historical values. As Megan Cassidy-Welch and Anne Lester observe, 'acts of remembering are always dynamic and relational. They involve processes of communication, reception and assimilation, all of which are shaped by the relationships we forge with each other and with the past'.[14] Indeed, it is the repetition itself which defines the relationship to which Cassidy-Welch and Lester allude.

UK Newspaper Crusades

In the context of the Little Crusader's troubled history and its championing of causes rooted in casual and banal nationalism, it is not at all surprising that on the occasion of their launch of the campaign to leave the European Union, it was immediately to the masthead logo of the little Crusader that the newspaper would turn. However, it is also not unsurprising that they should refer to their campaign as a crusade in itself, because it is by no means a term unique to the *Express*. It is surprisingly commonplace for newspapers, at least in the UK, to refer unflinchingly to an assortment of political, social or moral campaigns as 'crusades'.[15] In that sense, it is clear that when applied to the everyday campaigns of domestic policy, the term has passed from one which promotes howls of protest (as Holsinger documents)[16] to a form of banal medievalism which passes unnoticed in everyday discourse.[17]

The centre- to far-right discourse of the nation, in particular, shows little reluctance to brandish a term like 'crusade', as can be seen from the history of the Little Crusader and its deliberately provocative hijacking by Beaverbrook (and, later Lord Aitken who in 1995 deliberately revived the reference to the Little Crusader to tie his own political fortune to the wagon of Lord Beaverbrook, his great uncle). In her speech to the Conservative Party Conference in 1986, British Prime Minister Margaret Thatcher spoke in terms which would have been warmly approved by the *Express*'s Little Crusader when she defined popular capitalism as 'nothing less than a crusade to enfranchise the many in the economic life of the nation. We Conservatives are returning power to the people'.[18] As such, it is easy to see the extent to which a term like 'crusade' was already being tied into the politics of the centre-right and their rugged, individualistic neoliberalism in the pursuit of a Hayek-inspired self-determination.

The assertion of 'common sense', then, and the claim to be following the 'will of the people', can be seen to feed directly into the same rhetoric which underpins the British tabloids' fondness for crusades. Rather than nuanced debate, they speak to a universalised 'we'. Rather than accept reasoned and principled opposition, they railroad the arguments to imply an underpinning moral imperative to whichever position has been adopted, marginalising dissenting opinions as fanaticism and sedition. The *Express*'s crusade to leave the EU was often recalled in later reports, even when only tenuously related to EU policies. Just under two years later, for instance, on Saturday 27 October 2012, the newspaper published a front-page news item which highlighted their ongoing 'crusade' to get Britain out of the EU after a report seemed to endorse an anti-EU stance: 'The verdict [about financial recovery] delivers a crushing blow to *the Euro-fanatics who insist we cannot survive economically without Brussels*, while boosting the *Daily Express*'s crusade for Britain to quit the EU'.[19]

Like the *Express*, and competing for much of the same political ground, the *Daily Mail* has launched its own crusades in their effort to poach readership from among the indignant right. Over the same period (2012–20), the *Mail* has launched over a dozen separate crusades, including for 'fairer ISAs' (26 October 2012), better access to post-retirement cash annuities (25 July 2018), as well as a decade-long 'crusade' against plastic bags which in 2019 morphed into one which had (by implication) always included single-use plastic (2 July 2019). In the realm of sport, the *Mail* reported that England are on a crusade to 'save Test Match cricket all on their own' (17 June 2014). Bathetically, on 14 December 2016 reporter Dan Hyde announced his crusade to 'unearth the dastardly tricks stores play to make us pay more', such as redesigning a box of frozen ready meals in order to change its price.[20]

It is, of course, not only the preserve of the *Mail* and the *Express*. Indeed, on any given day British newspapers may readily be found at the helm of one crusade or another, and in this respect the UK's former Prime Minister Boris Johnson, himself previously an editor and columnist, could regularly be found launching crusades in the august tradition of indignant entitlement which is characteristic of Middle England. Over the course of only two months in 2014, for instance, Johnson launched a crusade to raise standards of accommodation (*The Evening Standard*, 4 June 2014), before embarking upon another crusade against diesel (*Independent*, 30 July 2014), and finally spearheading a crusade to save the Conservative Party (3 August 2014).

Neither do these crusades imply consistency and coherence. On 6 January 2011, London's *Evening Standard* reported that Johnson was on a 'personal crusade' to open another London airport in the east of the city. Three years later (in response to the *Evening Standard*'s own crusade for the third runway), Johnson launched a crusade *against* Heathrow growth, before carrying out another u-turn against his own crusade (*Daily Telegraph*, 18 July 2015). Three years later, as Foreign Secretary, he was conveniently out of the country and thus unable to vote on the official parliamentary debate on the third runway, refusing to oppose or support it. In February 2020, when the government's plans were defeated, Johnson again refused to comment on the cancellation of Heathrow's expansion.

Johnson's crusades were not limited to runways, of course. In the political turmoil of summer 2019, Johnson found the time to launch a crime fighting crusade (*The Guardian*, 12 August 2019). Four months later in January 2020, he could be found fighting a 'social care crusade' (*Daily Mail*, 15 January 2020). Four days after that he was on a 'crusade to "level up" the country' (*The Sun*, 19 January 2020), alongside an ongoing 'Ready to Trade' crusade in *The Sun* (2 January 2020), all the while supporting his former Brexit Secretary David Davis's 'crusade' against US Extradition treaties (*Mail on Sunday*, 20 February 2020) as well as, apparently, junior minister Jake Berry's own crusade to 'Save Our High Streets' in conjunction with the *Express*.[21] Throughout the Covid pandemic of 2020, Johnson and his government could be found waging crusades to keep schools open (*The Sun*, 9 June 2020), continuing the 'Brexit Crusade' (*The Herald*, 9 September 2020), launching a 'Green Crusade' (*The Telegraph*, 20 November 2020), and another to allow families to celebrate Christmas together (*The Sun*, 1 December 2020).

Brexit and Medievalism

In all of these competing (and often contradictory) crusades, what is clear is the extent to which the crusader – a banal medievalism in its invocation – becomes slowly and inexorably bound up within a complex network of meanings and competing subtexts according to their specific national, cultural and political contexts. As Mike Horswell argues in his study of crusading mentalities after the First World War, the revival of medievalism to map onto modernity renders both into a third element produced by the act of remembering: 'both were reimagined as they were revived'.[22]

With regard to medievalism, what does emerge clearly is how – and how easily – the medieval past signalled through the crusader becomes intertwined with an emerging rhetoric which strikes out in defiance of increasing European integration on the one hand and globalising rhetoric on the other. Beaverbrook's return to 'crusader medievalism' can be situated as his response to a perceived threat posed by a series of trade laws over which the UK seemed increasingly less in touch and less in control. As such, the connection between the Imperial Crusade and Beaverbrook as a British Establishment figure mirrors that of the EU and Brexit: in both circumstances, crusader medievalism becomes a banal medievalism stretched over the bones of the British Empire, as an indexical balm to sooth the furrowed brow of a pervasive nostalgia across a certain generation and political group.

Indeed, the rhetoric in the Houses of Parliament reflects precisely the fear which crusader medievalism assuages. In the four years since the EU referendum, the backbenches of the Conservative Party have been responsible for any number of rather interesting instances of banal medievalism in the invocation of a historical past to suggest a path for Britain's future.

Jacob Rees-Mogg could be found grasping at a series of historical straws to support his case for leaving the EU, such as his description of Alfred the Great as 'Britain's first Eurosceptic', and the description of Brexit as 'Magna Carta'. Many of his references require some rather simplified history in order to work, such as his classification of the Vikings as the European Union which then allowed him to introduce Kipling's line that 'if once you have paid him the Danegeld, you never get rid of the Dane'.[23]

Among the backbenchers, we are also able to find Daniel Hannan, who unflinchingly describes of the Battle of Hastings as England's Nakba (the Palestinian Exodus of 1948), a term which calamitously combines the medieval (Hastings) with the late twentieth century. It is also a sensitive reference, given the long-standing Israel-Palestine tensions, particularly since it is rooted in a subtle invocation of the kind of oppression involved in colonisation, a colonisation rooted in Sykes-Picot of 1916 and led, in part, by the British Empire itself. Amid Hannan's confusion, UKIP's then-leader Nigel Farage rode to the rescue, wearing a Bayeux Tapestry tie (*Mail Online*, 18 September 2018) in order to talk about 'England's' history of self-determination. For the confused, his reference to the Bayeux Tapestry was an allusion to 'the last time we were invaded and taken over', and so he thus reframed the EU as a Norman yoke, while also carelessly conflating England with Britain, a move guaranteed to irk the ten million Scottish, Northern Irish and Welsh nationals who make up the UK (and who mostly did not vote in favour of Brexit).

With medieval history suddenly up for grabs, Brexit's various medievalisms became fair game for all, in some cases with precisely the same medievalism being used for opposite purposes. In 2016, speculation over Theresa May winning the Conservative leadership led the *Evening Standard* to paint the anachronistic image of her 'sweep[ing] into Downing Street like Queen Boudica scything men down with her stilettos'.[24] A 2017 article in the Scottish *Daily Record* continued the analogy by calling her 'the Boudica of Brexit', though here it was intended as a criticism of her pursuit of a hard Brexit which was then, as now, unpopular in Scotland.[25] A year later, this time in the right-leaning broadsheet *The Telegraph*, Tory MP Michael Fabricant used precisely the same comparison for a complimentary interpretation, expressing an earnest desire that Prime Minister Theresa May become 'the new Boudicca', using a reference to the Celtic queen's rebellion against Roman occupation to imply a sense of longevity to British exceptionalism.[26] Indeed, less than a month after the *Telegraph* op-ed, Fabricant's odd comparison found itself repeated in the pro-Leave newspaper, *The Sun*, in which Nick Timothy – May's former Chief of Staff, who advised her early hard stance on Brexit – encouraged the Prime Minister to 'discover her inner Boudicca' in her negotiations with the European Union, including a graphic in which May's head was photoshopped onto the statue of Boudicca which stands at Westminster.[27] Also in 2018, researchers at UCL discovered a growing movement of those who described her political opponent, Nigel Farage, as 'a modern-day

Boudica, standing up to Jean-Claude Juncker's Nero', amid fierce online discussions about Brexit taking place on social media about modern parallels with Roman occupation.[28]

Other medievalisms were even more difficult to follow. In *The Telegraph* on 14 August 2018, Giles Fraser wondered aloud if Brexit would be the new Reformation. The left-wing *Guardian* chimed in with its pro-European reading of medievalism, offering 'King Canute's lessons for Brexit', (22 August 2016) which sees the spirit of Anglo-Danish co-operation as a model, and the futility of trying to stop the tide as a handy metaphor for the messy negotiations about Britain's exit from the EU. Never one to be outdone in a competition for obsolescence and obscurity, on Twitter (X) Rees-Mogg confused even the BBC's political editor with his rejection of the Chequers plan (a template for Britain's independent trade policies) as 'the greatest vassalage since King John paid homage to Philip II at Le Goulet in 1200'.[29]

A Perfect Storm

If it is true that the build up to the 2016 referendum as well as the Brexit fallout did indeed promote a new vocabulary of medievalism, then the question is not only why, but why should they do so specifically in that period? After all, with the exception of the chained crusader, there seem to have been no equivalent movements relating to the joining of the EU in 1973, so why were they raised in relation to leaving? The Maastricht Treaty to integrate Europe was signed in 1992, 40 kilometres away from Charlemagne's capital in Aachen, and yet no mention was made of it. The formation of NATO in 1949 and its enlargements in 1952–2020, the digging of the Channel Tunnel in the 1990s, or Britain's entry into the G6 in 1975: all of these movements have seen the UK joining and inevitably sharing power with other nation states, yet none of these seem to have engendered any significant medievalism surrounding loss of sovereignty. So why should Brexit invoke the crusades and medievalism so insistently?

The first answer lies in the function of Brexit itself. The referendum was offered not as a simple vote on membership, but an exploration of nationhood as a whole. The sentiment expressed by the crusader, for instance, is telling, in his claim that 'we *demand* our *country* back!'. No sensitive unpacking of nationalism or national ideologies here: what is powerful about the *Express*'s rather perfunctory claim is its use of 'we' as a powerful universal subject of national belonging, constructed ad hoc as an implicit in-group with which a marginally less implicit out-group can be juxtaposed. It is for this reason that the specifically English cliffs of Dover should be transmuted into a generically British border with Europe.

This use of an imaginary anti-European crusade reflects a fundamentally different understanding of the term outside of academic discourse which offers an unwittingly ironic confirmation that the crusader of populist xenophobia is emphatically not the same crusader being discussed in academia. 'A recent trend', Horswell argues, 'in medieval scholarship has been to recognise the crusades as being intrinsically bound up with medieval European society'.[30] Amid its non-scholarly usage outlined above, the meaning of crusade is more or less directly the reverse. Crusades like those above are increasingly bound up with assumed, flattened out identity politics in the English-speaking press which in the UK rely on an underpinning sense of British exceptionalism and self-determination.

Thus, the potential power of regular crusades against banal targets does not require its believers to agree about the choice of target, but it instead becomes a kind of modern, secular papal bull. By invoking the crusades, when crusading has been re-imagined to frequently to imply something which Middle England should be against, the meaning of the term has been emptied. As Horswell observes, 'the crusades are often a marker of what popularly defines "medieval", existing prominently in what one commentator has labelled "the permanent anachronistic stew" of the "medieval imaginary"'.[31]

A crusade in the *Express* thus rallies the ruddy-cheeked indignation of Middle England, validating their perceived victimhood on behalf of the marginally affronted, uniting the imaginary community of 'right-minded' readers in outrage under a similarly imaginary banner.

To rephrase that more simply, the 'we' implied by the *Express*'s term 'our country' presupposes a united group of those who actively belong to and possess the heritage on display (namely the cliffs, the birds, the knight, and the crusades, but also the defiance underpinning it all). Its power, of course, is also rooted in the opposite: it also reclaims that heritage by presupposing an out-group made up of those who seek to threaten those values and to whom none of those historically British elements belong. Both are entirely invented. The rhetorical stance of 'we demand' is thus a perfect illustration of the universal subject of belonging upon which any theory of nation relies, and it becomes an imaginary in-group which always invents the 'our country' on which it is built.

Brexit's medievalism thus offered a reconfiguration of the medieval roots of nationhood as nothing less than a referendum on nationality, reframing complex and imaginary questions about national sovereignty into a simplified 'in/out' group, wherein the Self is the 'we' who demand 'Our Country' back and any dissenters are suspiciously foreign. The rhetoric both pre- and post-Brexit can thus be seen to rely on what Anthony D. Smith calls a nationalism of *ethnie* and not *patrie*, wherein 'the presumed boundaries of the nation are largely determined by the myths and memories of the dominant *ethnie*, which include the foundation charter, the myth of the golden age and the associated territorial claims, or ethnic title-deeds'.[32]

It is not a question of contributing or constructing a nation, but it is a question about remembering heritage, recovering the imagined past, and defending an entirely invented national tradition. The medievalism of Brexit is thus, ironically, both exclusionary and nostalgic and also, at the same time, dependent entirely on a powerful group of media moguls who are able to repeat invented medieval traditions.

In its invocation of medieval heritage intertwined with English national identity, the invented tradition of the crusader thus perfectly aligns with Smith's model of constructed national identity:

> [One] way of constructing maps and moralities for present generations was through the use of history and, especially, the cult of golden ages. *The purposes of nationalist educator-intellectuals are social and political, not academic*; they aim to purify and activate the people. To do so, moral exemplars from the ethnic past are needed, as are *vivid recreations of the glorious past of the community. Hence the return to the past through a series of myths*: myths of origins and descent, of liberation and migration, of the golden age and its heroes and sages, perhaps of *the chosen people now to be reborn after its long sleep of decay* and/or exile. Together, these myth-motifs can be formed into a composite nationalist mythology and salvation drama.[33]

And this is why for a political project like Brexit to work, it needs the participation of its readers, whether that participation is registered through coupons, through votes, or through a toxic drip-feed of misinformed historical memory. It needs the participatory consensus that medieval England/Britain are expressions of a somehow unique and righteous empire. Moreover, it needs a project which believes that the British Empire was not only right, good and natural, but that it was inevitable, and unequivocally benefitted its colonial subjects.

The invocation of the Middle Ages through the crusader is thus a way of claiming the crusades as English, reframing them as defensive,[34] and blurring the border between the past and the present, pretending that the medieval past inheres in the present rather than defining the extent to which is differs from it. It is a way of intermingling the temporal planes by recalling a past overlaid on successive layers of pastness, transforming a geopolitical conflict into a temporal one. It is a way of sidestepping debates about the future by falling back on tired renegotiations of a past. It is also, finally, about power, and who gets to control those images.

In a frantic media return of the medieval, these kinds of banal medievalisms are often so overdetermined, so meaningful, that they conflict with the broader rhetoric. The invocation by Farage, for instance, of the Bayeux Tapestry, seemed to confuse even the *Daily Mail*.[35] As their headline struggled to wrest a bad pun about 'cutting ties to Europe' (Farage was wearing a tie featuring the Bayeux Tapestry) from the confusing message, their rhetorical question and the extent to which the pun does not work demonstrates what Peter Catterall has called 'studied ambiguity', a meaninglessness which is laying bare the extent to which meaning is up for grabs.[36]

These medievalisms, by not meaning anything, are thus divested of meaning, laying them open to any kind of ideological hijack. The Middle Ages, in the context of the fraught terrain of banal medievalism, are *made to mean*, rather than being inherently meaningful. In an unwitting continuation of Barthes, the death of the author and the death of an expert both combine here to create floating signifiers ripe to be grafted onto any convenient and passing cultural myth. Given the ideological hijack of the Little Crusader to contain all manner of petty microaggressions enacted against an entitled and indignant Middle England, perhaps a future cartoon might see armies of medievalists lined up along Fleet Street waving spears vaguely at the offices, *demanding* their crusades back.

Notes

1 'Get Britain Out of the EU', *Daily Express*, 8 January 2011.

2 Mike Horswell, *The Rise and Fall of British Crusader Medievalism, c.1825–1945* (Abingdon, 2018), p. 4.

3 Harold D. Clarke, Matthew J. Goodwin, and Paul Whiteley, *Brexit* (Cambridge, 2017); Beatrice Heuser, *Brexit in History: Sovereignty or a European Union?* (Oxford, 2019); Benjamin Martill and Uta Staiger (eds), *Brexit and Beyond: Rethinking the Futures of Europe* (London, 2018).

4 I have also analysed this front cover from the perspective of political medievalisms and Brexit more generally in my essay, 'Medievalism, Brexit, and the Myth of Nations', *Studies in Medievalism* 29 (2020), pp. 31–8.

5 'Sour Grapes from Italy over Claims That Prosecco Rots Teeth', *Daily Mail*, 1 September 2017. Admittedly, the quotation was from Luca Zaia, the Lega Nord president of the Veneto region, but my point is that even if an Italian far-right politician is fuzzy about the chronological details, a national British newspaper should see the problems inherent in the idea that Anglo-Saxons were fighting crusades.

6 Patrick J. Geary, *The Myth of Nations: The Medieval Origins of Europe* (Princeton, NJ, 2002); Eric J. Hobsbawm and Terence O. Ranger, *The Invention of Tradition* (Cambridge, 1992).

7 Tim de Lisle, 'Little Crusader Rides Again', *The Independent*, 16 April 1995, p. 9. Emphasis my own.

8 Roy Greenslade, *Press Gang: How Newspapers Make Profits from Propaganda* (London, 2004), p. 64.

9 de Lisle, 'Little Crusader Rides Again'.

10 Robert Frank Dewey, *British National Identity and Opposition to Membership of Europe, 1961–63: The Anti-Marketeers* (Manchester, 2009), ch. 2.

11 Dewey, *British National Identity and Opposition to Membership of Europe*, p. 71.

12 Dewey, *British National Identity and Opposition to Membership of Europe*, p. 39.

13 In Peircean semiotics, an index is a specific kind of sign which points to the existence or presence of something else, like the waving flag points to the existence of wind (2.275). A symbol, however, only points back to the original object through general agreement (2.449). For a good overview, see Winfried Nöth, *Handbook of Semiotics* (Bloomington, 1995), pp. 44–5.

14 Megan Cassidy-Welch and Anne E. Lester, 'Memory and Interpretation: New Approaches to the Study of the Crusades', in *Crusades and Memory: Rethinking Past and Present*, ed. Megan Cassidy-Welch and Anne E. Lester (Abingdon, 2017), p. 3.

15 Andrew B.R. Elliott, *Medievalism, Politics and Mass Media: Appropriating the Middle Ages in the Twenty-First Century* (Woodbridge, 2017), pp. 78–90. See also

Cassidy-Welch and Lester, 'Memory and Interpretation', or Horswell, *British Crusader Medievalism*.

16 Bruce Holsinger, *Neomedievalism, Neoconservatism, and the War on Terror* (Chicago, 2007).

17 Elliott, *Medievalism*, p. 15ff.

18 Margaret Thatcher, Speech to Conservative Party Conference, 10 October 1986, p. 26. The speech is archived at the Margaret Thatcher Foundation's website <https://www.margaretthatcher.org/document/106498> [accessed 30 November 2020].

19 Martyn Brown, 'Britain's Economy Too Good For EU', *The Express*, 27 October 2012, p. 1. Emphasis my own.

20 'It Might Be the Season of Goodwill - but Don't Expect any from Your Insurer', *Thisismoney.co.uk*, 14 December 2016 <https://web.archive.org/save/https://www.thisismoney.co.uk/money/article-4030398/It-season-goodwill-don-t-expect-insurer-says-Dan-Hyde.html> [accessed 15 January 2023]. For more examples of crusades, and particularly the ways in which they are self-contradictory, see Elliott, *Medievalism*, pp. 87–90.

21 David Williamson, 'Minister Vows He Will Revive Our High Streets', *Sunday Express*, 26 January 2020, p. 6.

22 Mike Horswell, 'Crusader Medievalism and Modernity in Britain', *Studies in Medievalism* 25 (2016), p. 25.

23 These examples are taken from a report in *The Irish Times* written by Christopher Kissane, tellingly entitled 'Historical Nonsense Underpins UK's Brexit Floundering', 17 September 2018, *Irish Times* <https://www.irishtimes.com/opinion/historical-nonsense-underpins-uk-s-brexit-floundering-1.3630936> [accessed 15 January 2020].

24 Melanie McDonagh, 'Genius of Theresa May Be Her Dull Anglican Ways', *The Evening Standard*, 12 July 2016, p. 15.

25 'Misdirection by Boudica of Brexit', *Daily Record & Sunday Mail*, 4 March 2017, p. 8.

26 Michael Fabricant, 'Incompetent? Theresa May Could Still End Up as a New Brexit Boudicca', *The Telegraph*, 5 September 2018 <https://www.telegraph.co.uk/politics/2018/09/05/incompetent-theresa-may-could-still-end-new-brexit-boudicca/> [accessed 21 April 2019].

27 Nick Timothy, 'It's Your Boudicca Moment, Theresa', *The Sun*, 16 October 2018, p. 10.

28 Mark Bridge, 'Farage Is Boudica to Europe's Emperors, Say Cyberwarriors', *The Times*, 10 April 2018, p. 19. The *Norwich Evening News* ran a story about the emergence of the Norfolk Independence Party, a group of around 120 residents of the county who supported 'Nexit' – the county's proposed departure from the UK. Their justifications included the suggestion that 'Norfolk sustained itself throughout history and did just fine in medieval times and in the days of Boudica. It's time for Nexit'. '"Forget Brexit We Need Nexit": Radical Call for Norfolk to Leave UK', *Evening News (Norwich)*, 21 February 2020.

29 Parliamentary speech tweeted by BBC Political Editor Laura Kuenssberg, 12 July 2018.

30 Horswell, *British Crusader Medievalism*, p. 12.

31 Horswell, *British Crusader Medievalism*.

32 Anthony D. Smith, *National Identity* (London, 1991), p. 39.

33 Smith, *National Identity*, p. 66. Emphasis my own.

34 For more on this process, see Horswell, *British Crusader Medievalism*; *Crusades and Memory*, ed. Cassidy-Welch and Lester; Mattias Gardell, 'Crusader Dreams: Oslo 22/7, Islamophobia, and the Quest for a Monocultural Europe', *Terrorism and Political Violence*, 26 (2014), pp. 129–55; and particularly Andrew Fiala, 'Crusades, Just Wars, and the Bush Doctrine', *Peace Review: A Journal of Social Justice*, 19 (2007), pp. 165–72.

35 James Curran and Jean Seaton, *Power without Responsibility: Press, Broadcasting and the Internet in Britain* (London, 2010), p. 51; see also Martin Pugh, *Hurrah for The Blackshirts! Fascists and Fascism in Britain between the Wars* (New York, 2013); Stephen Dorril, *Blackshirt: Sir Oswald Mosley and British Fascism* (London, 2017).

36 Peter Catterall, "'Efficiency with Freedom?' Debates about the British Constitution in the Twentieth Century", in *Reforming the Constitution: Debates in Twentieth-Century Britain*, ed. Peter Catterall, Wolfram Kaiser and Ulrike Walton-Jordan (Abingdon, 2014), p. 34.

Bibliography

Primary

Bridge, Mark. 'Farage Is Boudica to Europe's Emperors, Say Cyberwarriors'. *The Times*, 10 April 2018, p. 19.

Fabricant, Michael. 'Incompetent? Theresa May Could Still End Up as a New Brexit Boudicca', *The Telegraph*, 5 September 2018. https://www.telegraph.co.uk/politics/2018/09/05/incompetent-theresa-may-could-still-end-new-brexit-boudicca/.

'"Forget Brexit We Need Nexit": Radical Call for Norfolk to Leave UK'. *Evening News (Norwich)*, 21 February 2020.

de Lisle, Tim, 'Little Crusader Rides Again'. *The Independent*, 16 April 1995, p. 9.

McDonagh, Melanie. 'Genius of Theresa May Be Her Dull Anglican Ways'. *The Evening Standard*, 12 July 2016, p. 15.

'Misdirection by Boudica of Brexit'. *Daily Record & Sunday Mail*, 4 March 2017, p. 8.

'Sour Grapes From Italy Over Claims That Prosecco Rots Teeth'. *Daily Mail*, 1 September 2017.

Timothy, Nick. 'It's Your Boudicca Moment, Theresa'. *The Sun*, 16 October 2018, p. 10.

Williamson, David. 'Minister Vows He Will Revive Our High Streets'. *Sunday Express*, 26 January 2020, p. 6.

Secondary

Cassidy-Welch, Megan, and Lester, Anne E., eds. *Crusades and Memory: Rethinking Past and Present*. Abingdon: Routledge, 2017.

Catterall, Peter, Kaiser, Wolfram and Walton-Jordan, Ulrike, eds. *Reforming the Constitution: Debates in Twentieth-Century Britain*. Abingdon: Routledge, 2014.

Clarke, Harold D., Goodwin, Matthew J., and Whiteley, Paul. *Brexit*. Cambridge: Cambridge University Press, 2017.

Conboy, Martin. *Tabloid Britain: Constructing a Community through Language*. London: Taylor & Francis, 2006.

Curran, James, and Seaton, Jean. *Power without Responsibility: Press, Broadcasting and the Internet in Britain*. London: Routledge, 2010.

Dewey, Robert F. *British National Identity and Opposition to Membership of Europe, 1961–63: The Anti-Marketeers*. Manchester: Manchester University Press, 2009.

Dorril, Stephen. *Blackshirt: Sir Oswald Mosley and British Fascism*. London: Thistle Publishing, 2017.

Elliott, Andrew B.R. *Medievalism, Politics and Mass Media: Appropriating the Middle Ages in the Twenty-First Century*. Woodbridge: D.S. Brewer, 2017.

Fiala, Andrew. 'Crusades, Just Wars, and the Bush Doctrine'. *Peace Review: A Journal of Social Justice* 19 (2007), pp. 165–72.

Gardell, Mattias. 'Crusader Dreams: Oslo 22/7, Islamophobia, and the Quest for a Monocultural Europe'. *Terrorism and Political Violence* 26 (2014), pp. 129–55.

Geary, Patrick J. *The Myth of Nations: The Medieval Origins of Europe*. Princeton, NJ: Princeton University Press, 2002.

Greenslade, Roy. *Press Gang: How Newspapers Make Profits from Propaganda*. London: Pan Macmillan, 2004.

Heuser, Beatrice. *Brexit in History: Sovereignty or a European Union?* Oxford: Oxford University Press, 2019.

Hobsbawm, Eric J., and Terence O. Ranger. *The Invention of Tradition.* Cambridge: Cambridge University Press, 1992.

Holsinger, Bruce. *Neomedievalism, Neoconservatism, and the War on Terror.* Chicago: Prickly Paradigm Press, 2007.

Horswell, Mike. 'Crusader Medievalism and Modernity in Britain'. *Studies in Medievalism* 25 (2016), pp. 19–28.

Horswell, Mike. *The Rise and Fall of British Crusader Medievalism, c.1825–1945*. Abingdon: Routledge, 2018.

Martill, Benjamin, and Staiger, Uta, eds. *Brexit and Beyond: Rethinking the Futures of Europe*. London: UCL Press, 2018.

Nöth, Winfried. *Handbook of Semiotics*. Bloomington: Indiana University Press, 1995.

Pugh, Martin. *Hurrah for the Blackshirts! Fascists and Fascism in Britain between the Wars*. New York: Random House, 2013.

Smith, Anthony D. *National Identity*. London: Penguin, 1991.

4 One Foot in Europe and the Other in Dixie

Neo-Confederates, Holy War, Chivalry, and the Crusades

Daniel Wollenberg

Calling itself the 'Political Voice of White Christian America', *The Crusader*, a newspaper published by the Ku Klux Klan, styles its readers as Christian knights, as Klan members have since the nineteenth century, defending what they deem to be the spirit and values of their ancestors. The Klan has long been idealised by its white supremacist members and supporters as a fortified bastion of chivalric masculinity protecting a beleaguered and disrespected Southern way of life; today, there are multiple Klan organisations that call themselves some variation of 'white knights'. They style themselves as 'knights' because they purport to protect white Christian families and communities from racial, religious, ethnic, and political outsiders, all of whom are seen as an inherent threat to the bogus fantasy of traditional Southern ways.

Thomas Dixon, Jr, whose racist novel *The Clansman* (1905) was adapted into the film *Birth of a Nation* (1915), infamously lionised the riders of the Klan as a thin chivalric line between civilisation and anarchy in his works – which is to say, for Dixon, between white supremacy on the one hand and racial justice and the equality of all Americans under the law on the other. In his novels, Dixon does not merely imply or vaguely point towards his penchant for white supremacy. He shouts it out loud. In *The Leopard's Spots* (1902), a naïve northern ingenue like Helen Lowell, just returned from her first trip south, might view chivalry as the alluring manliness of young Southern white men who care little for Northern trifles like money and exhibit 'such knightly deference! Such charming old-fashioned chivalrous ways!'[1] But the narrator knows better than Helen. He wants us to see southern chivalry as more than an enchanting façade. He wants us to see it for what it truly is: a crucial barrier protecting white privilege and power from racial and gender egalitarianism. Immediately after a Black youth is lynched by the Klan and hanged from

DOI: 10.4324/9781003033035-5

the balcony of the courthouse, the narrator gives thanks to the Klansmen by recounting their origins across the South:

> It was the answer to their foes of a proud and indomitable race of men driven to the wall. In the hour of defeat they laid down their arms and accepted in good faith the results of the [Civil War]. And then, when unarmed and defenceless, a group of pot-house politicians for political ends, renewed the war, and attempted to wipe out the civilisation of the South.
>
> This Invisible Empire of White Robed Anglo-Saxon Knights was simply the old answer of organised manhood to organised crime. Its purpose was to bring order out of chaos, protect the weak and defenceless, the widows and orphans of brave men who had died for their country, to drive from power the thieves who were robbing the people, redeem the commonwealth from infamy, and re-establish civilization.[2]

The Klan, moving out from the shadows of night into the open sunshine of a daytime parade, has struck deathly fear and terror into every Black citizen of the town of Hambright. White power has been re-entrenched; the next chapter is titled 'How Civilization Was Saved'. These are medieval crusading knights come back to life to defend Christendom anew. In Dixon's *The Traitor* (1907), as a woman gazes with awe upon a Klansman on horseback with crusader-style red crosses painted on his robe, she exclaims, 'The spirit of some daring knight of the middle ages come back to earth again!'[3] And in the novel *The Clansman*, the narrator dreams wistfully of the medieval as he points the camera at Klansmen:

> The moon was now shining brightly, and its light shimmering on the silent horses and men with their tall spiked caps made a picture such as the world had not seen since the Knights of the Middle Ages rode on their Holy Crusades.[4]

Then, they bind and gag a Black man and are thanked by whites for their service to the community.

Despite being over a century old, the excerpted passage from *The Leopard's Spots* still reflects some of the major ideas and canards of neo-Confederates today, both in the KKK and in other white supremacist groups. Many of these hope to be thought of as incarnations of chivalric Christian soldiers defending 'civilisation' against outsiders, both infidels and Americans of colour alike; as men on 'their Holy Crusades', engaging in a noble and morally right struggle. Twenty-first-century neo-Confederates, fashioning themselves as Christian soldiers defending America and Western civilisation, maintain a way of thinking that can be traced from the mid-nineteenth century which holds that the US Civil War (1861–65) was a holy war fought between the pious South and the heretical or atheistic North. That holy war is portrayed in neo-Confederate thought as having been fought to defend authentic Christian traditionalism in the South, and Southern soldiers then and neo-Confederate activists and extremists now are often portrayed in neo-Confederate rhetoric and imagery as holy warriors. The crusades, as a series of Christian holy wars, are thus aligned in neo-Confederate thought – sometimes explicitly and at other times implicitly – with the US Civil War.

This chapter argues that the Civil War is positioned in neo-Confederate thought as a modern crusade, and that views of the crusades as necessary defences of Christian homelands, rather than as aggressively invasive Catholic wars against Muslims, Jews, pagans, and heterodox Christians, are grafted by neo-Confederate apologists onto the Civil War. The rhetoric of holy war, pious soldiers, heretics, and infidels that was deployed during the Civil War continues to proliferate among neo-Confederates. My aim here is not to offer a comprehensive account of the crusades and neo-Confederacy. While there are discussions and examples offered of neo-Confederates explicitly drawing on the crusades and crusader imagery, at some moments I will draw a line connecting the crusades and the Civil War as having similar semantic structures in Confederate and neo-Confederate rhetoric. The crusades will be addressed directly at times; elsewhere, a broader parallel between medieval holy war and the Civil War will be invoked. The end goal of both approaches is to suggest that for neo-Confederate thought, the Civil War plays a similar role that the crusades have played for the far and extreme right in the US, Europe, and Australia.

Neo-Confederate Holy War

Neo-Confederacy is a spectrum of beliefs from a relatively broad range of groups and individuals without a unified, singular vision or message. At its core, to be a neo-Confederate is to be an apologist for the Confederacy. Neo-Confederacy arose in the decades after the end of the Civil War and has had resurgences at various points in the last century; at each point, it reflects historical revisionism in its nostalgia for an Old South that was hierarchical, deeply Christian, and that offered social harmony for all, with whites in power and Black slaves content to be permanently and forcibly subjected to poverty, suffering, and violence. In short, neo-Confederates' core set of beliefs are grounded in the Lost Cause myth,[5] white nationalism, white heritage, states' rights, and what they would view as 'traditional' Christian values.[6]

The term 'neo-Confederate' essentially describes any apologist for the Confederacy after the end of the Civil War and the dissolution of the Confederate States of America. In its broadest application, neo-Confederacy entails any embrace of the Confederacy, from wearing a Confederate flag patch or otherwise displaying the battle flag to defending the myth of the Lost Cause in any capacity. The most intense, explicit neo-Confederate discourse today espouses outright racism, hate-fuelled violence, and full-blown calls for another

Southern secession from the union. Neo-Confederacy covers a broad spectrum of beliefs, but white supremacy and white nationalism are constant elements on the spectrum. There have been a few key surges of neo-Confederate activity in the past century and a half, most notably the 1890s, the 1920s, and currently, since the mid-1990s. In the last 25 years, neo-Confederates typically also espouse virulent anti-Islamic, anti-Semitic, racist, sexist, and homophobic beliefs, or they align with groups and individuals who do so.

As people who self-style as defenders of 'traditional' Christian values, the crusades – or to be more precise, a common misrepresentation among those on the political right of the crusades as a necessary defence of Christendom against aggressive Islamic armies – are a logical historical point for neo-Confederates to latch onto. Crusaders – at least popular conceptions of them – combine two crucial elements that neo-Confederates revere: displays of Christian piety and red-blooded masculinity, embodied in the image of the crusader knight. The most well-known neo-Confederate 'knights' – those of the Ku Klux Klan – intentionally style their costumes to look generally like medieval Templars, with the so-called Blood Drop Cross, a white cross set on a red background, stitched onto white robes. Since the nineteenth century, continuing an argument made before and during the Civil War by slave owners and proponents of the chattel slavery system, many neo-Confederates have interpreted the Civil War as a holy war between true Christian soldiers and the heretical Union army, and many neo-Confederates – especially a secessionist hate group like the League of the South (discussed later) – perceive and project themselves as Christian soldiers fighting against a godless secular enemy.

The 'theological war thesis' suggested by Edward Sebesta and Euan Hague, that the Civil War was a holy war at its core, can be found from the mid-nineteenth century onwards in the thought of both slave owners and proponents of the theological war thesis today, in two interconnected ways. Firstly, that it was fought for the correct interpretation of the Bible – in short, that both the Hebrew Bible (the Old Testament) and the New Testament condone slavery – and against the Bible's misinterpretation in abolitionists' claims that the Bible condemns slavery. Secondly, supporters of the theological war thesis envision the Civil War as a holy war between true Christians and godless infidels, a battle between good (the slaveholding South) and evil (the abolitionist North), between God's army and its enemies. Although Lincoln in his second inaugural address famously said that both North and South 'read the same Bible, and pray to the same God; and each invokes His aid against the other', both Northern and Southern writers during the war unsurprisingly assumed that God was on the side of their righteous cause.[7] Both positions were grounded in the theological questions concerning slavery, as both northern and southern writers saw the institution respectively as either an unholy evil or a sacred institution accepted by Scripture.

Some Southern clergymen and writers in particular, however, viewed the war as a holy war both during it and long after its conclusion, and Confederate soldiers were, and continue to be, canonised as holy warriors. The myth of what Charles Reagan Wilson calls the Crusading Christian Confederate 'taught Southerners to crusade against evil, to bear the suffering which accompanied that struggle, and to die in Christian faith'.[8] Idealising the Confederate soldier as a crusader has played a crucial role in the promulgation of the Lost Cause myth, allowing apologists for the Confederacy to frame the Civil War as a struggle for virtue, and thus as merely one chapter in an ongoing struggle for virtue and morality against a materialistic, industrial, secular North. In turn, the Confederate soldier who died in the war is perceived by neo-Confederates as having died not in vain but rather as a martyr on the front lines of a spiritual struggle that continues to this day.

Confederate propaganda demonised the Union army as a brute force capable only of wanton violence and the Confederate army as a collection of pious chivalric heroes.[9] A southerner writing in her diary at the start of the war reflects the tenor of this propaganda: 'This war has fully brought out and developed the peculiar dispositions of both North and South, how poorly does the thieving, burning, murdering Yankee compare with the generous, chivalrous Southerner'.[10] In a poem composed in Fort Warren in 1862, a Confederate spoke of the crusading southern soldier with rapture:

> Doing battle, like a knight,
> 'Gainst a host in a stricken field;
> Trebly armed by sense of right,
> Christ's red cross upon his shield.[11]

Both North and South were viewed by many southern writers of the mid-nineteenth century in monolithic terms, with innate northern and southern profiles that were endemic and that ensured permanent rifts between populations that were often characterised as being fundamentally disparate. One nineteenth-century South Carolinian preacher named James Henley Thornwell notoriously saw abolitionists as the enemies of order and the Bible, and the battle between slaveholders and abolitionists as a life-or-death struggle between Christianity and atheism. 'The parties in this conflict are not merely Abolitionists and Slaveholders', Thornwell writes in a well-known quote, but

> Atheists, Socialists, Communists, Red Republicans, Jacobins on the one side, and friends of order and regulated freedom on the other. In one word, the world is the battleground, Christianity and Atheism the combatants, and the progress of humanity the stake.[12]

For Thornwell, slavery was an institution accepted by the Bible and was thus not an open moral question, so to condemn slavery as fundamentally immoral is to attack the word of God. Put simply, then, the Civil War was for Thornwell essentially a battle between Christians and infidels. The North's foremost fight was not against states' rights or against the institution of slavery, but primarily against the Christian faith itself.

Slaveholder Chivalry – Justifying Violence

Developing in the late twelfth century, especially in courtly romances such as those of Chrétien de Troyes, and generally remaining a vital set of values for the nobility until about 1500, chivalry was, in the European Middle Ages, more an assortment of notions about loyalty, protection of those in need of protection, piety, virtue, magnanimity, and martial prowess than a specific order or code that can be strictly defined.[13] Chivalry did not develop in exact lockstep with the crusading ideal, but the Church's push to justify and elevate religious violence in the later eleventh century and the campaigns of the Second and Third Crusades through the next century likely did impact chivalry's insistence on the merits of ethical violence. Chivalry was more an ideal that flourished in medieval romance than in practice, and from the beginning it was contested and problematic: for example, in Marie de France's lai *Milun*, composed in the second half of the twelfth century, the chivalric ideal is placed into direct conflict with familial and marital obligations, as knights seek fame and renown at the expense of their responsibilities to their families. Despite the ugliness of chivalry in reality – violence, however justified, can only be such – the romantic fantasy of the armed knight on horseback riding for God, king, and country flourished during the period of the crusades. In his *Life of Saint Louis* (written 1305–09), an encomium for Louis IX of France, Jean de Joinville lauds the king as an ideal knight who embodies the ideals of honourable violence and Christian virtue, encouraging his knights to defend the faith with the sword against all enemies while maintaining the peace among Christians, remaining generous in arms, devout in worship, just in all things, and supportive of the poor.[14] That fantasy of violent piety endured well beyond the Middle Ages. Its potent combination of courage, strength, loyalty, generosity, and humility made the chivalric fantasy part of the foundational sense of what it meant to be a gentleman in a place like the American South. Chivalry worked to justify violence in the name of higher ideals.

The core beliefs of neo-Confederates today about masculine physical strength, female purity, honour, a rigid social hierarchy, and chivalry were cultivated in the nineteenth century by white southerners inspired by the Middle Ages.[15] These 'medieval' values, as white southerners saw them, promoted moral certainty and were in contradistinction to the individualistic and godless North, which promoted moral relativity. It was common for white Southerners in the nineteenth century, as well as twentieth-century scholars sympathetic to neo-Confederacy and the Lost Cause myth, such as Richard Weaver and Eugene Genovese, to link proclamations about honour and nobility among chivalric white Southerners with the chivalry of medieval knights. The medieval ideal of chivalry has long been cast as playing a fundamental role in shaping the values of the white Southern gentleman, and both the nineteenth-century South and medieval western European societies were idealised by Confederates and neo-Confederates as being virtuous and idealistic at their core, despite the absurdity of making such an argument about a society that permitted the enslavement of humans. For Genovese, nineteenth-century southerners shared with chivalric knights the desire to combine 'gentleness, humility, and fierceness in battle', and he sees chivalry, primarily the protection of white women and the disempowered, as a civilising force that white Southerners inherited from medieval knights.[16] Without those chivalric ideals, Genovese argues, slaveholders would have been even more inhumane. Even if southern soldiers 'often failed to live up to their professed standards', so did chivalric knights in the crusades, who professed to walk a Christian path while not always staying on it; Genovese quotes Gibbon on crusader knights having 'neglected to live, but [who] were prepared to die, in the service of Christ'.[17] However, just because the ideal was not always practised does not mean that we should dismiss the 'effect of the chivalric ideal on the lives of white men who aspired to fame or simply to think of themselves as decent'.[18] In this account, chivalry is thus accepted as a flawed but crucial component of the white, male, Southern mindset, and character. All things considered, the Confederate soldier and the slaveholder alike really were, for Genovese, bastions of chivalric values that were a throwback to a time long past.

Southern clergymen in the nineteenth century claimed that the Confederate soldier embodied the glories of chivalry and moral duty, like Louis IX in Joinville's text or as Arthur and his knights did in some foggy mythical past, the legends of which were routinely alluded to in southern writings.[19] The Civil War was envisioned as a moral crusade that worked to ennoble Confederate soldiers as holy Christian warriors. Reverend J.L. Underwood wrote in 1906:

> The inspiration of the knightly hearts of the Confederacy was home and the inspiration of a pious home was godly woman. The world will never know how effective were the prayers and letters of the women at home in those great religious revivals with which the Confederate army was so often and so richly blessed. Thousands of men who entered the army wicked men went home or to their graves genuine Christians.[20]

The secession of southern states from the Union was viewed by some Confederates as a reflection of God's will and an act of chivalry. One Georgia clergyman declared, 'I look upon the secession of the southern states as the grandest, most noble and chivalrous, patriotic and God-like achievement ever effected by any oppressed people in the world', and an Alabama preacher proclaimed that 'it is doing God service to kill the diabolical wretches on the battlefield'.[21] Many soldiers in both armies felt that they were sanctimonious Christian soldiers fighting with God on their side, but one of the persistent core tenets of the myth of the Lost Cause today is that the Southern army consisted of devout, chivalric Christian soldiers fighting against atheism and heretics, and that contemporary white Southern identity continues to be the last bastion of authentic Christianity in the United States.

Neo-Confederates and apologists today for the slaveholding South accept and defend nineteenth-century proclamations from southern writers about the inherently chivalric nature of the Southern gentleman. The slaveholder often envisioned himself as a chivalric gentleman, believing that Christianity fostered respect for women and a paternalistic relationship between both master and slave, and husband and wife. Slaveholders saw chivalry as placing limits on the excesses and inhumanity of holding humans as slaves, just as it limited wanton brutality in warfare. They idealised chivalry and the chivalric gentleman to cover their inhumane and immoral actions as slaveholders. Proclamations about Confederate gentility and chivalry were – and remain – ultimately bogus justifications papering over the brutal atrocities of slavery in America. Whether wilfully cruel or blind and deaf to the abhorrence of their actions, many male slaveholders perceived themselves as knightly, Christian men guarding idealised women and protecting the right to hold slaves. According to an account by Genovese and Elizabeth Fox-Genovese, many slaveholders could not see the loathsome barbarism of their words and deeds and envisioned themselves as knightly, Christian gentlemen upholding chivalric virtues, especially by protecting their women.[22]

The Genoveses shape a narrative of the southern gentleman slaveholder that has been advanced by advocates and apologists for the Confederacy since the mid-nineteenth century, as the notion of the chivalric Christian soldier or gentleman holding the line against a heretical or atheistic enemy informs a major aspect of the Lost Cause myth. For neo-Confederates today like the League of the South (LS), which is a white supremacist, secessionist, neo-Confederate hate group whose postings declare white Southern moral and cultural superiority over other regions of the US and non-white, non-Christian Americans, opposition to the Confederate States of America (CSA) and to memorials and remembrances of the Confederacy are seen as an implicit rejection of Christianity. The LS sees the fundamental purpose of the CSA not as a military force defending a state whose primary motive for secession was the maintenance of slavery, but as a security force for the defence of the Christian faith in the United States.[23] This contemporary deployment of the theological war thesis is used as a justification by LS for a renewed secession of Southern states from the US and the establishment of a white, Christian ethnostate. The Civil War as a theological war – as a holy war – is one of the enduring elements of the Lost Cause myth, as it continues to be foundational to neo-Confederates' visions of the key legacy of white southern exceptionalism, especially among 'heritage' organisations and publications.[24] Writing at the turn of the century for the Chalcedon Foundation, a Christian Reconstructionist organisation designated as a hate group by the Southern Poverty Law

Center for its anti-LGBT views, Steve Wilkins, a neo-Confederate apologist for chattel slavery and a founding member of the LS, claims that the Confederacy was 'the last bastion of Christendom' and he calls for the modern South to reject 'the false gods of humanism' and to re-embrace the 'godly culture' of a pre-Enlightenment West.[25]

Contemporary Neo-Confederacy

The mid-1990s saw a new wave of neo-Confederate activity that continues two decades later. Aligned against multiculturalism, gay rights, civil rights laws, immigration, secularism, the removal of the Confederate flag and Confederate statues and monuments from public spaces and, more recently, the Black Lives Matter movement, neo-Confederates in the twenty-first century are an agglomeration of Agrarian romantics yearning for a 'simpler time', libertarians, racists, and Christian soldiers (of course, these groups are not always exclusive of each other).[26] These 'Christian soldiers' see the South as a God-centred society that is the last refuge of traditional Christianity and rejects secular ideas and values, and they perceive a divide between North and South today that is much the same, in their view, as the theological foundations of the Civil War. Once the purview of neo-Confederates academics and scholars, the theological war thesis filtered into mainstream neo-Confederate thought in the 1990s and became a status quo position about the Civil War.[27]

One neo-Confederate blogger, a member of the Sons of Confederate Veterans, writing on the website of the Abbeville Institute, a right-wing organisation formed in 2003 which generally sees white Americans as a disempowered, aggrieved group and promotes what it views as the 'achievements' of the South, recently proclaimed that for neo-Confederates today, their 'Cause' is the same as the white southern cause in 1861.[28] This blogger's post claimed that for Stonewall Jackson the Civil War was a 'Crusade, a holy war waged on behalf of the Lord'; Jackson was a true soldier, and the Confederate army was God's army. In this blogger's view, Jackson helped transform the Confederate army into a pious, law-abiding Christian fighting force:

> Not since the Crusades had anything like this [turning the Confederate army into a Christian army] occurred', he writes, 'and we certainly have no examples after our Cause was lost. This proxy war between God and Satan is fully exposed when we compare the conduct of our soldiers of the cross with the vicious rapine and plunder of our brutal enemy.

In a flamboyant and maudlin prose style that is common to neo-Confederate writings, the blog entry ends with racist fearmongering about undocumented immigrants and laments that the same divide exists today between North and South as in 1861, imploring southerners to 'keep the faith and carry the fire' against the northern enemy.

The Civil War and the supposedly unbridgeable divide between northerners and southerners serve as evidence, for neo-Confederates, of an endless holy war between God's chosen people and heretics. At the 85th anniversary of the dedication of the Arlington Confederate Monument in 1999, a member of the Sons of Confederate Veterans gave a speech in which he praised the Confederacy as 'the last real Christian civilization on earth' and conceived of the Civil War as a holy war between infidels and true believers: 'There was indeed a profound difference in theology between the North and the South in antebellum America. The Northern intellectual leadership preached a heretical and socialist Gospel. The South held on to a robust, traditional, Trinitarian Christianity'.[29] During the Civil War, 'God brought forth among the Southern armies the greatest revival of religious faith in the history of the United States'. In racist terms, the neo-Confederate's speech promoted core falsifications of the Lost Cause myth, particularly that slaves were happy to be enslaved and lived good lives as unfree people, and called for the South and the US as a whole to return to the moral virtues of the Confederacy. Although both the North and South during the war believed that God would grant them victory and that they were on the side of right, Confederates saw the war as a struggle between true Christians and rationalist atheists.

This interpretation of the war continues to be widely held among neo-Confederates. One influential figure for the modern neo-Confederate movement, M.E. Bradford, wrote in the early 1990s,

> As the War approached, [Southern] clergymen more and more tended to view the sectional controversy as a dispute between those who acknowledged the authority of the Scripture and those who set their own moral sense above it – in other words, between Christians and infidels.[30]

Christian Reconstructionists increasingly collaborated with neo-Confederates in the 1990s, and the theological war thesis became entrenched as a core part of the ideology of neo-Confederate groups like the LS. Sebesta and Hague argue that this collaboration over the past three decades between the Christian Reconstructionist movement and secessionist extremists like the LS is evidence of 'a conflation of conservative, neo-Confederate and Christian nationalisms into a potent reinterpretation of United States history, one centred upon the thesis that the Confederate states were a bastion of orthodox Christianity standing in the face of the heretical United States'.[31]

In the past 25 years, neo-Confederate extremists have embraced the framework of an unbridgeable religious divide between North and South. The white supremacist politics of Identity Dixie, a secretive, far-right secessionist group, and the LS are extremist points on the long historical arc of the Lost Cause myth and the view among neo-Confederates that the Civil War was a holy war. The theological war thesis is deployed by contemporary white neo-Confederate hate groups as a never-ending racial and cultural war between Christian chivalric soldiers against 'assaults' by the left; in this warped view of American politics, it is white southerners – or rural white Americans in general – who are a targeted group while ethnic, racial, and religious minorities enjoy endless unearned privileges. The LS, which began as the Southern League in 1994, was originally comprised of a small group of southern academics, but in the ensuing decades the LS has become explicitly racist, sexist, Islamophobic, and anti-Semitic.[32] As white nationalists, the LS' primary goal is the secession of the southern states from the US in order to found an independent white ethnostate. The new Confederate nation would consist of 15 states, including four states that were not part of the original CSA (Kentucky, Missouri, Maryland, and Oklahoma).

Even if the LS had a veneer, however thin, of a respectable academic sheen at its inception, the group was transparently racist from the start and the founding members' white nationalist and white supremacist beliefs are not difficult to perceive. In 'The New Dixie Rights Manifesto', published by the *Washington Post* in 1995 and written by two of LS' founding members, Michael Hill and Thomas Fleming, it is entirely obvious that the manifesto, when it speaks about 'the mind of the South', 'authentic cultural traditions', or 'culture and language', is obviously referring to white Christians.[33] When Hill and Fleming lament 'what our people have suffered', they are not addressing the millions of Black Americans who suffered the indescribable pain, torture, and oppression of being enslaved for centuries, but are alluding to a fantasy about northern desires to dominate – culturally, politically, religiously, economically – white southerners. Hill and Fleming call this desire for northern domination 'cultural genocide'. The manifesto proclaims that the South has its own unique (white) identity and that, under the banner of states' rights, they just want to be free to live their lives as they see fit. That culture is a Christian one:

> [W]e take our stand squarely within the tradition of Christianity. This historic faith, though everywhere attacked by the hollow men of modernity, has always been central to the pursuit of personal honor, political liberty, and human charity. Asking for only the religious freedoms guaranteed in the Bill of Rights, we oppose the government's campaign against our Christian traditions.

The manifesto's conclusion is thus a clear articulation of one important part of the Lost Cause myth: that the generally accepted and accurate truth of the Civil War – that it was fought over the institution of slavery, which was the bedrock of the southern agrarian economy – was not the real cause of the war. Hill's and Fleming's manifesto suggests that the Civil War and the ongoing religious and political divide between North and South are fundamentally battles over states' rights and against a tyrannical federal government, and that the war continues to be fought by pious white Christian soldiers.

The LS insists that the South is fundamentally and constitutionally different from mainstream American culture primarily because of its embrace of conservative, 'historic' Christianity, thus positing a cold holy war between the 'hollow men of modernity' and Christian traditionalists fighting under the banner of the Cross.

Medievalism is a key aspect of the LS' conception of what it means to be southern. Southern society, their website proclaims, 'perpetuates the chivalric ideal of manhood – respect for, and protection of, our women, and the development of the virtues of honesty, courage, honor, and humility'.[34] Clearly influenced by commonly held views both at the time and now of white southern gentlemen in the nineteenth century as the perpetuators of medieval chivalry, the LS views the white southern man as a beacon of honour and a necessary, respectful protector of white women and children. The medievalism of the LS is taken further by the LS' Virginia chapter, which makes grandiose, paranoiac claims about the intentions of the political left and that describes the 'struggle' between the South and its perceived enemies in terms of a holy war and crusade: 'Our culture is being sacked by an unholy crusade of leftist agitators and foreign relations and our very physical survival depends on us organizing and effectively defending ourselves from this enemy who seeks to eliminate us from the planet earth'.[35] Their struggle is existential, fought against an enemy who wants to see their entire culture eradicated: 'This is why it is absolutely imperative that we rally what is left of our people, our resources, and every last vestige of Western Civilization in Dixie; to stand together and secure a future in which OUR culture can survive, dominate and thrive'. For the LS, there is a war being perpetually waged against white Southerners. The word 'crusade' is applied by the LS to an incorrigible northern and leftist desire to abolish slavery in the nineteenth century and to eradicate a white southern way of life today, but it is clear that the Christian, chivalric soldiers are white southern males fighting against godless and heretical forces.

Crusader imagery is deployed by other neo-Confederate groups in order to make the case that neo-Confederates today are the same militaristic forces as crusader knights eight centuries ago. Identity Dixie, has two subgroups for special members: the Knights of the Silver Circle and the Knights of the Golden Circle. The crusades are depicted by an Identity Dixie post entitled 'The Nature of our Blood' as a unifying rallying call for Christians against Saracens, whose primary goal, they claim, was to wipe out Christendom. But Christians – by which the post clearly means whites – must unite: 'When we unite, under Christ and with iron discipline, no malignant force can stand against us, just like those knights of old, who in Jerusalem's dark and desperate hour defeated a Saracen army many times greater in strength'.[36] Warfare is the 'natural state' of white Christians: 'Our ancestors were barbarians, crusaders, monks, agrarians, explorers, merchants, knights, and conquerors. And that same blood, which still flows through our veins and is constrained by the modern world, is begging to be free'. That blood flows through white southern veins. As a white Identitarian group Identity Dixie advertises itself as 'the true Sons of the South, bound by a shared history and culture and united common vision'; by shared history, Identity Dixie means that of their medieval 'ancestors' such as the Celts, the Normans, and the Anglo-Saxons and embracing medievalism – a patriarchal, 'traditional household', 'a sense of community' – while rejecting 'modernism'.[37] Neo-Confederates today construct a critical link between the perceived advantages of the premodern world and the perceived disadvantages of the modern world. In neo-Confederate thought, the South is the heir to premodern European social structures that were '"naturally" hierarchical, patriarchal, racially determined, and far superior to the present'.[38] The South, in this view, is a monolithic, timeless extension of the idealised static world of the European Middle Ages, which featured masculine, chivalric, Christian soldier-knights ready to defend their homes and families at all costs.

Heritage medievalism is a crucial component of contemporary neo-Confederate discourse. Sons of Confederate Veterans are a 'heritage' group that formed in the late nineteenth century whose primary purposes are historical revisionism and white identity politics, painting the Confederacy in a positive light and protecting Confederate monuments and symbols. In its first two sentences, the SCV's charter document names the Magna Carta as being crucial to the political foundations of the United States. The US Constitution is 'the very Magna Carta of our liberties', and the SCV declares that as an organisation they 'adhere to the principles of the Great Charter of England granted at Runnymede, A.D. 1215, and the Anglo-Saxon rights and personal liberties transmitted to us thereunder'.[39] Chivalry is portrayed as a fundamental attribute of the Confederacy, passed down through the generations: 'Confederate ancestors [...] by their sacrifice, perpetuated unto us and our descendants that glorious heritage of valor, chivalry and honor which we now hold and venerate'. Similarly, the LS, in their 'Core Beliefs Statement', proclaims that white southern society 'perpetuates the chivalric ideal of manhood'.[40] They claim to be part of a 'long community of blood' stretching back before the white settling of America to northern and western Europe, especially the British Isles.

Conclusion

There is not a fine line between neo-Confederacy and white supremacy in America, as the two are inextricably linked and intertwined. There is unsurprising overlap between neo-Confederates and extreme right-wing anti-government militias whose members regularly espouse white supremacist beliefs. Formed in 2008, the Three Percenters are a far-right, anti-government militia movement whose members often open-carry long rifles in public spaces as a show of intimidation, and in doing so, demonstrate that enmeshing. The Virginia Task Force of Three Percenters nicknames their group the 'Dixie Defenders'. At far and extreme-right rallies and gatherings, the Confederate flag and crusader and medieval-style icons and symbols fly alongside each other. Confederate battle flags with 'III' – the Three Percenters logo – emblazoned on them are common, and the Confederate flag is regularly displayed at Three Percenter rallies and protests. Three Percenter gear is also rife with medievalism, as they brand themselves on their t-shirts, patches, stickers, hats, and licence plate holders with 'Crusader' imagery. Along with other neo-Confederate far-right groups like the Heritage Preservation Association that sport logos with medieval helms, a significant portion of Three Percenter gear shows off medieval-style imagery: t-shirts with the hallmark III on a 'Crusaders Cross', or Jerusalem cross; hoodies with the III on a 'Crusader Shield'; patches that read 'Pork Eating Crusader' with a red-eyed Knight Templar devouring a piece of pork; Deus Vult patches. There is a Three Percenter patch that reads, 'Time for another Crusade'. An American firearms manufacturer sells a rifle it calls the Crusader, which is named 'to hoist the flag of our faith and to make a statement […] The war is here. We have a duty to defend our homeland and our way of life'. This Crusader rifle is sold alongside another rifle called Black Assassin. Two types of symbols – the Confederate flag and crusading – form part of the same white nationalist projection of embattled victimhood for rural white Americans eager to project themselves as Christian soldiers fighting the long battle for 150 years. But we should not discount these images as merely puerile fantasies. In 2016, the FBI arrested three Kansas men who were members of a militia group connected to the Three Percenters on conspiracy charges, for having plotted to blow up buildings that are home to many Muslim immigrants. They called themselves 'The Crusaders'.[41]

The Confederate battle flag and the crusader's cross are part of the same matrix of white resentment and fatuous projections of a 'people' under siege from nefarious outside forces, which are variously cast as 'cultural Marxists' and Black Americans to Muslims and Jews. In a long historical arc traced by the far and extreme American right, the crusades and the Civil War serve a similar political agenda. The deployment of the crusades and crusader rhetoric and imagery by white supremacists in the US, Europe, and Australia is likely well known both to medievalists and to the general public by now, from Anders Breivik claiming to be a Templar terrorist, to the Australian terrorist who murdered 51 people at two mosques in Christchurch, New Zealand, with rifles that had medieval dates, names, and tropes etched into them, to the Unite the Right rally in Charlottesville, Virginia, in 2017, where makeshift shields and armour with medieval-style imagery were used by neo-Nazis and the extreme right.

In contradistinction to a leading crusades scholar like Christopher Tyerman, who insists on the necessity of making sharp distinctions between medieval and contemporary conflicts, for white supremacist extremists, the crusades are mischaracterised as a necessary defence of Christian Europe from militant invaders.[42] In this revisionist view, the crusades are aligned with anti-immigrant movements and they are co-opted to serve as a model for how

Western nations today ought to 'defend' themselves against perceived outsider threats of non-white, non-Christian immigrants, and migrant workers. At its core, this view of the crusades – as a necessary, essential defence of Christendom that was vital in protecting a 'civilized' way of life – is similar to the way that the Civil War is portrayed by neo-Confederate apologists for the South.

In a sense, the crusades are pitched by contemporary white supremacists in a similar way as the American Civil War was by Confederates and continues to be by neo-Confederates: as a necessary defence of a white, Christian way of life against godless or heretical invaders seeking to destroy their traditions, heritage, and religion. This is a revisionist, white supremacist interpretation of the Civil War. In other words, both the crusades and the American Civil War are favourably cast in these schemas as crucial defences of white power under siege. Even if both the crusades and the Civil War were lost causes, their symbolism of pious militancy remains vital for those who look to the past to justify their hate and their violence. Comparing far-right rhetoric about the crusades with neo-Confederate rhetoric about the Civil War demonstrates how similar the roles are that both conflicts play for some on the political fringes. At far-right political rallies, on online forums, and at anti-immigrant marches, Confederate and crusader symbols and outfits both proliferate. The costumes and symbols and memes have become so prevalent that in early 2020, even Donald Trump Jr – son of the then-US president, who defended the Mississippi state flag that contained a Confederate battle flag[43] – was photographed flaunting a rifle with a so-called crusader's cross emblazoned on it.[44]

Notes

1 Thomas Dixon, Jr., *The Leopard's Spots: A Romance of the White Man's Burden – 1865–1900* (1902) <https://www.gutenberg.org/files/54765/54765-h/54765-h.htm> [accessed 13 February 2020].

2 Dixon, *The Leopard's Spots*.

3 Thomas Dixon, Jr., *The Traitor: A Story of the Fall of the Invisible Empire* (1907) <http://www.gutenberg.org/files/54766/54766-h/54766-h.htm> [accessed 13 February 2020].

4 Thomas Dixon, Jr., *The Clansman: An Historical Romance of the Ku Klux Klan* (1905) <http://www.gutenberg.org/files/26240/26240-h/26240-h.htm> [accessed 12 February 2020].

5 The Lost Cause began to be articulated in the years after the end of the Civil War by Confederates and their sympathisers and it can still be heard in some corners of contemporary political rhetoric today. It is a pseudohistorical myth that tries to shape and influence public remembrance of the war effort as an honourable, just, worthy cause. The actual cause of the Civil War for secessionist states – the continuance and protection of the institution of slavery, which was the foundation of a Southern agrarian economy – was not the real cause of the war, according to the Lost Cause myth. Instead, it holds that the Civil War was waged by the South to defend states' rights against a tyrannical federal government, fought in order to protect a Southern way of life that was threatened by northern finance, industry, and aggression.

6 For a general overview of neo-Confederacy, see 'Neo-Confederate', *Southern Poverty Law Center* <https://www.splcenter.org/fighting-hate/extremist-files/ideology/neo-confederate> [accessed 15 January 2020].
7 Abraham Lincoln, 'Second Inaugural Address' (1865), *The Atlantic* <https://www.theatlantic.com/past/docs/issues/99sep/9909lincaddress.htm> [accessed 9 June 2020].
8 Charles Reagan Wilson, *Baptized in Blood: The Religion of the Lost Cause, 1865–1920* (Athens, GA, 1980), p. 57.
9 For a study of the vilification of the North by Confederate propagandists, see George C. Rable, *Damn Yankees! Demonization and Defiance in the Confederate South* (Baton Rouge, LA, 2015).
10 Mary L. Mackall, Stevan F. Meserve, and Anne Mackall Sasscer (eds), *In the Shadow of the Enemy: The Civil War Journal of Ida Powell Dulany* (Knoxville, TN, 2009), p. 14.
11 G.W.B., 'Lines Written in Fort Warren', in *The Southern Poems of the War*, ed. Emily V. Mason (Baltimore, 1868), p. 224.
12 James Henley Thornwell, *The Collected Writings of James Henley Thornwell* (Richmond, VA, 1873), pp. 405–06.
13 Maurice Keen, *Chivalry* (New Haven and London, 2005), pp. 1–17.
14 See Joinville and Villehardouin, *Chronicles of the Crusades*, trans. M.R.B. Shaw (New York, 1963), pp. 175, 337, 348.
15 See Ritchie Devon Watson, Jr., *Normans and Saxons: Southern Race Mythology and the Intellectual History of the American Civil War* (Baton Rouge, LA, 2008), p. 51.
16 Eugene Genovese, 'The Chivalric Tradition in the Old South', *The Sewanee Review*, 108 (2000), p. 196.
17 Genovese, 'The Chivalric Tradition in the Old South', p. 201.
18 Genovese, 'The Chivalric Tradition in the Old South', p. 201.
19 Wilson, *Baptized*, p. 39.
20 J.L. Underwood, *The Women of the Confederacy* (1906), *The Gutenberg Project* <https://www.gutenberg.org/files/36969/36969-h/36969-h.htm#INTRODUCTION_TO_WOMANS_WORK> [accessed 10 June 2020].
21 Quoted in George C. Rable, *God's Almost Chosen People: A Religious History of the American Civil War* (Chapel Hill, NC, 2010), pp. 53, 68.
22 Elizabeth Fox-Genovese and Eugene D. Genovese, *The Mind of the Master Class: History and Faith in the Southern Slaveholder's Worldview* (Cambridge, 2005), pp. 337–8.
23 Edward H. Sebesta and Euan Hague, 'The US Civil War as a Theological War: Neo-Confederacy, Christian Nationalism, and Theology', in *Neo-Confederacy: A Critical Introduction*, ed. Euan Hague, Heidi Beirich, and Edward H. Sebesta (Austin, TX, 2008), p. 52.
24 For a synopsis of the arc of the theological war thesis from the mid-nineteenth century to the early twenty-first century, see Edward H. Sebesta and Euan Hague, 'The US Civil War as a Theological War: Confederate Christian Nationalism and the League of the South', *Canadian Review of American Studies/Revue canadienne d'etudes américaines*, 32 (2002), pp. 253–79.
25 Steve Wilkins, 'Christianity, the South, and the Culture War', *Chalcedon Foundation* <https://chalcedon.edu/magazine/christianity-the-south-and-the-culture-war> [accessed 6 June 2020].
26 Christopher M. Centner, 'Neo-Confederates at the Gate: The Rehabilitation of the Confederate Cause and the Distortion of History', *Skeptic*, 9 (2002), pp. 60–66.
27 Sebesta and Hague, 'The US Civil War as a Theological War: Confederate Christian Nationalism', p. 269.

28 Neil Kumar, 'Charge! And Remember Jackson', *The Abbeville Blog* <https://www.abbevilleinstitute.org/blog/charge-and-remember-jackson/> [accessed 10 April 2020].
29 Alistair C. Anderson, 'Address at Arlington National Cemetery', *Arlington Cemetery* <http://www.arlingtoncemetery.net/anderson-address.htm> [accessed 24 February 2020].
30 M.E. Bradford, 'The Theology of Secession', *Abbeville Review*, Abbeville Institute <https://www.abbevilleinstitute.org/review/the-theology-of-secession> [accessed 15 May 2020].
31 Sebesta and Hague, 'The US Civil War as a Theological War: Confederate Christian Nationalism', p. 267.
32 'League of the South', *Southern Poverty Law Center* <https://www.splcenter.org/fighting-hate/extremist-files/group/league-south> [accessed 3 February 2020].
33 Michael Hill and Thomas Fleming, 'The New Dixie Rights Manifesto: States' Rights Shall Rise Again', *Washington Post* <https://www.washingtonpost.com/archive/opinions/1995/10/29/the-new-dixie-manifesto-states-rights-shall-rise-again/d4abec20–6e0c-4733-b1d7-db2f60d1b8ab/> [accessed 6 March 2020].
34 'Core Beliefs Statement of the League of the South', *The League of the South* <https://leagueofthesouth.com/corebeliefs/> [accessed 24 April 2020].
35 'The Virginia League of the South', *The League of the South* <https://leagueofthesouth.com/the-virginia-league-of-the-south/> [accessed 16 March 2020].
36 'The Nature of our Blood', *Identity Dixie* <https://identitydixie.com/2020/04/17/the-nature-of-our-blood/> [accessed 25 June 2020].
37 'About', *Identity Dixie* <https://identitydixie.com/about/> [accessed 25 June 2020].
38 Kevin Hicks, 'Literature and Neo-Confederacy', in *Neo-Confederacy: A Critical Introduction*, p. 227.
39 'The Constitution of the Sons of Confederate Veterans', *Sons of Confederate Veterans* <https://scv.org/wp-content/uploads/2019/08/SCV-CONSTITUTION-2019.pdf> [accessed 6 March 2020].
40 Core Beliefs Statement of the League of the South', *The League of the South* <https://leagueofthesouth.com/corebeliefs/> [accessed 24 April 2020].
41 Jessica Pressler, 'The Plot to Bomb Garden City, Kansas', *New York Magazine* <https://nymag.com/intelligencer/2017/12/a-militias-plot-to-bomb-somali-refugees-in-garden-city-ks.html> [accessed 25 August 2020].
42 See, for example, Christopher Tyerman, *God's War: A New History of the Crusades* (Cambridge, MA, 2007), p. xiv.
43 Scott Simmons, 'Donald Trump Jr. supports tradition of Mississippi flag', *WAPT* <https://www.wapt.com/article/donald-trump-jr-supports-tradition-of-mississippi-flag/2099058> [accessed 13 January 2020].
44 Sarah Pulliam Bailey, 'Donald Trump Jr. poses with rifle decorated with a cross used during the Crusades', *Washington Post* <https://www.washingtonpost.com/religion/2020/01/06/donald-trump-jr-poses-with-rifle-decorated-with-cross-used-during-crusades/> [accessed 7 January 2020].

Bibliography

Primary

'The Constitution of the Sons of Confederate Veterans'. https://scv.org/wp-content/uploads/2019/08/SCV-CONSTITUTION-2019.pdf.

'Core Beliefs Statement of the League of the South'. *The League of the South*. https://leagueofthesouth.com/corebeliefs/.

Dixon, Jr., Thomas. *The Clansman: An Historical Romance of the Ku Klux Klan*. www.gutenberg.org/files/26240/26240-h/26240-h.htm.

Dixon, Jr., Thomas. *The Leopard's Spots: A Romance of the White Man's Burden – 1865–1900*. www.gutenberg.org/files/54765/54765-h/54765-h.htm.

Dixon, Jr., Thomas. *The Traitor: A Story of the Fall of the Invisible Empire*. www.gutenberg.org/files/54766/54766-h/54766-h.htm.

Lincoln, Abraham. 'Second Inaugural Address' (1865). *The Atlantic*. www.theatlantic.com/past/docs/issues/99sep/9909lincaddress.htm.

Thornwell, James Henley. *The Collected Writings of James Henley Thornwell*, vol. IV. Richmond, VA: Presbyterian Committee of Publication, 1873.

Underwood, J.L. *The Women of the Confederacy*. www.gutenberg.org/files/36969/36969-h/36969-h.htm

'The Virginia League of the South'. *The League of the South*. https://leagueofthesouth.com/the-virginia-league-of-the-south/.

Secondary

Anderson, Alistair C. 'Address at Arlington National Cemetery'. www.arlingtoncemetery.net/anderson-address.htm. [Accessed 24 February 2020].

Bradford, M.E. 'The Theology of Secession'. *The Abbeville Review*. www.abbevilleinstitute.org/review/the-theology-of-secession. [Accessed 15 May 2020].

Centner, Christopher M. 'Neo-Confederates at the Gate: The Rehabilitation of the Confederate Cause and the Distortion of History'. *Skeptic* 9 (2002), pp. 60–6.

Fox-Genovese, Elizabeth and Genovese, Eugene D. *The Mind of the Master Class: History and Faith in the Southern Slaveholder's Worldview*. Cambridge: Cambridge University Press, 2005.

Genovese, Eugene. 'The Chivalric Tradition in the Old South'. *The Sewanee Review* 108 (2000), pp. 188–205.

Hicks, Kevin. 'Literature and Neo-Confederacy'. In *Neo-Confederacy: A Critical Introduction*, ed. Euan Hague, Heidi Beirich and Edward H. Sebesta. Austin: University of Texas Press, 2008, pp. 226–52.

Hill, Michael and Fleming, Thomas. 'The New Dixie Rights Manifesto: States' Rights Shall Rise Again'. *Washington Post*. www.washingtonpost.com/archive/opinions/1995/10/29/the-new-dixie-manifesto-states-rights-shall-rise-again/d4abec20-6e0c-4733-b1d7-db2f60d1b8ab/.

Joinville, Jean de and Villehardouin, Geffroy de. *Chronicles of the Crusades*, trans. M.R.B. Shaw. New York: Penguin Books, 1963.

Keen, Maurice. *Chivalry*. New Haven, CT: Yale University Press, 1984. Reprint, New Haven, CT: Yale University Press, 2005.

Kumar, Neil. 'Charge! And Remember Jackson'. *The Abbeville Blog*. https://www.abbevilleinstitute.org/blog/charge-and-remember-jackson/.

'League of the South'. *Southern Poverty Law Center*. https://www.splcenter.org/fighting-hate/extremist-files/group/league-south.

Mackall, Mary L., Meserve, Stevan F., and Sasscer, Anne Mackall, eds. *In the Shadow of the Enemy: The Civil War Journal of Ida Powell Dulany*. Knoxville: University of Tennessee Press, 2009.

'Neo-Confederate'. *Southern Poverty Law Center*. https://www.splcenter.org/fighting-hate/extremist-files/ideology/neo-confederate.

Pressler, Jessica. 'The Plot to Bomb Garden City, Kansas'. *New York Magazine*. https://nymag.com/intelligencer/2017/12/a-militias-plot-to-bomb-somali-refugees-in-garden-city-ks.html.

Pulliam Bailey, Sarah. 'Donald Trump Jr. Poses with Rifle Decorated with a Cross Used during the Crusades'. *Washington Post*. www.washingtonpost.com/religion/2020/01/06/donald-trump-jr-poses-with-rifle-decorated-with-cross-used-during-crusades/.

Rable, George C. *God's Almost Chosen People: A Religious History of the American Civil War*. Chapel Hill: University of North Carolina Press, 2010.

Rable, George C. *Damn Yankees! Demonization and Defiance in the Confederate South*. Baton Rouge, LA: Louisiana State University Press, 2015.

Sebesta, Edward H. and Hague, Euan. 'The US Civil War as a Theological War: Confederate Christian Nationalism and the League of the South'. *Canadian Review of American Studies/Revue canadienne d'etudes américaines* 32 (2002), pp. 253–79.

Sebesta, Edward H. and Hague, Euan. 'The US Civil War as a Theological War: Neo-Confederacy, Christian Nationalism, and Theology'. In *Neo-Confederacy: A Critical Introduction*, ed. Euan Hague, Heidi Beirich and Edward H. Sebesta. Austin: University of Texas Press, 2008, pp. 50–75.

Simmons, Scott. 'Donald Trump Jr. Supports Tradition of Mississippi Flag'. *WAPT*. www.wapt.com/article/donald-trump-jr-supports-tradition-of-mississippi-flag/2099058.

Tyerman, Christopher. *God's War: A New History of the Crusades*. Cambridge, MA: Belknap Press, 2007.

Watson, Jr., Ritchie Devon. *Normans and Saxons: Southern Race Mythology and the Intellectual History of the American Civil War*. Baton Rouge, LA: Louisiana State University Press, 2008.

Wilkins, Steve. 'Christianity, the South, and the Culture War'. *Chalcedon Foundation*. https://chalcedon.edu/magazine/christianity-the-south-and-the-culture-war.

Wilson, Charles Reagan. *Baptized in Blood: The Religion of the Lost Cause, 1865–1920*. Athens: University of Georgia Press, 1980.

5 Knives in the Dark and the Death of History

Validating the Far-Right's Middle Ages through *Assassin's Creed*

Thomas Lecaque and Joshua Call

A mysterious figure in white, looking down on an execution in a square from a bell tower. That same figure, wandering through the crowd. Three Hospitallers killed in rapid succession, before the figure must flee through the crowded streets of a crusader city. Trapped by guards, he escapes by blending in with white-robed monks, as the game screen loads: *Assassin's Creed.* Released in 2007 on console and 2008 on PC, *Assassin's Creed* was an award-winning game at the Electronic Entertainment Expo in 2006 and 'greatly outstripped' the sales expectations of Ubisoft, its French video game company publisher.[1] It spawned a series that now includes 11 main games, 11 further spin-off games, a live-action film starring Michael Fassbender, three short films, a list of graphic novels, a book series, and a concert series.[2] As of September 2022, the *Assassin's Creed* franchise had sold over 200 million games.[3] That first game, set during the Third Crusade (1187–92) and setting up a millennia-spanning story of conflict between Templars and Assassins, built a narrative of crusader conspiracies and hidden treasures that, while entertaining, mythologised a medieval past built upon not just shaky historical ground, but an actively harmful vision of a mythic, conspiratorial past. That neomedieval past is not only a post-enlightenment vision of an occult world divorced from actual religion but, we contend, a dangerous collection of ideologies of the mythic Middle Ages. By constructing such a world for gamers to imprint their own ideologies into, *Assassin's Creed* played an important role in the genesis of alt-right game spaces, which, in turn, gave birth to GamerGate and contemporary neo-fascist groups. To understand this means considering the representational complexity of the game as a media artefact, and the difficulty that readers/players encounter parsing historical fact from the much more entertaining world of historiographic metafiction. Digital games like *Assassin's Creed* are primed for their ability to tell us interesting fictional stories but understanding how readers fail to distinguish fact from fiction while engaging them is a vital task.

DOI: 10.4324/9781003033035-6

Representations vs. Remediations: Games as History

It is difficult to overstate the currency for discussing historical representation in the contemporary moment. Indeed, this chapter is being drafted against a backdrop of both academic and layperson argument about multiple historical narratives. Popular media continues to leverage conspiracy theory-laden entertainment in ways that reinforce the mistaken assumptions of an audience broadly uninformed by actual historical fact. In and of itself, this is not necessarily troubling – entertainment and academic study are, after all, distinct endeavours. Tom Apperley is quick to remind us that one of the most popular genres that emerged in the twentieth century was that of 'alternative history', which resulted in the adaptation of the genre's tropes into multiple popular media formats.[4] While these adaptations are entertainingly popular, their ability to colour our historical lenses often effaces our understanding of what history is, how it unfolded, and the spectrum of possibilities that such study might afford us. This is especially true when we consider the role of games as an interactive experience.

As a beginning point for this work, we should be clear that games are not synonymous with history. They are commercial entertainment, a representational medium, bound to sets of rules, and subject to the interpretations of designers and players. It is not an uncomplicated definition. After all, in a strict sense, what sets this idea apart from the very concept of history? Historical narratives are, by definition, narratives – subject to the interpretations, contingencies, and contexts of how they are constructed. There is considerable support for the idea that digital games are an effective way to engage in the representation of historical forms; they promote engagement with historical consciousness by pointing to the possible similarities between game design and the process of historians.[5] This is a somewhat radical shift, suggesting that a teleological approach might offer us something different from an epistemic one. After all, both history and historical narratives are determined by 'the selection of facts, which concedes that here we are limited not only by those facts selected by the historian, but also by which facts are available in the first place, which ones are known, and which facts are assumed'.[6]

The work that games engage with is similar but distinct from that of historical construction. The representational processes between these two distinct modes of meaning making are, at least philosophically, related. And games do afford a valuable historical lens for conceptualising historical narratives. To think about history means to think in terms of events and implications, a connected series of events whose construction unfolds as a kind of contextual consequentialism. Game studies see this as an opportunity for engaging in 'counterfactual history', a notion that challenges the tendency of the multiple contingencies of the past being homogenised into a singularity in hindsight. Unlike the literary genre of alternative history, it provides a legitimate historical approach to the speculation on how events might have otherwise occurred.

This notion permits a plural approach to the past, each past is still an interpretation, but they are no longer necessarily hegemonic.[7]

This enforces a complexity to the consequentialist lens that laypeople often bring to historical thinking by positing an evolving and complicated series of 'What if?' questions. Such thinking is critical to a careful analysis of both historical events and contemporary associations and appropriations of history more broadly. But this framework, while a logical extension of humanities in general, does seem distinct from the aim of strict historical investigation. It is game-focused, rather than history-focused. And this is a distinction worth highlighting when there is significant disciplinary overlap given the often-interdisciplinary work of people engaged in digital humanistic inquiry.

Such moves are understandable given the representational work of digital games. *Assassin's Creed* has taken great pains to present itself as a compelling piece of historical fiction without offending 'religious sensibilities'.[8] Both the game's designers and its critically aware audience are keenly aware of how multiple media enterprises have constructed both representations of the Middle East, and the iconography of the crusades, and the relative success of the franchise in avoiding the 'ethnical stereotypes of "the Arabs"'[9] makes it both compelling and a relative standout compared to other media form. The entire franchise takes great pains to inform viewers that the team employs diverse designers. The opening splash screen advises us that 'Inspired by historical events and characters. This work of fiction was designed, developed and produced by a multicultural team of various religious faiths and beliefs'.[10] This is a twofold rhetorical move. It presents an ethos that positions a studio above reproach for being inclusive. Unfortunately, it also carries a significant implication for how players read the content of the game. Because the studio employs cultural consultants, players read the constructions and creations with an air of gravitas not warranted for such fictional works. To wit, real people made this, so the objects that reflect the real-world cultural images of this diverse team must also be real because to be factually incorrect would be problematic or offensive. It's an interesting twist when doing the right thing for good reason sometimes simultaneously produces bad ends.

This rhetorical framework is aided by a significant degree of fidelity to the player's ideas about the game, its narrative, and geography. This then, is the central complication of *Assassins Creed's* historical fiction. It 'feels' real. It accomplishes this through its careful manipulation of narrative and thematic tropes that contribute to its believed fidelity. There is significant scholarship detailing how the representational practices of historical games are generated and delivered through aesthetics that are exceedingly westernised, culturally translated, and narratively mediated.[11] These tropes are a cultural carryover that originates in assumptions made through a lens of fiction that builds on just enough history to be believable – a counterfactual history rendered through the game's design. Through the constant reinforcement of these tropes, the fictional depictions gradually replace the historical reality. This is

Baudrillard's nightmare made substance – 'reality has passed completely into the game of reality'.[12]

And this is the trap of neomedievalism. The representational practices are more real than real, so they supplant any concept of real in the player's mind. This is what transmedia scholars would refer to as remediation, a practice where 'the recycling of existent media is a way of strengthening the new medium's claim to immediacy' that also 'remind[s] the viewer of the presence of the medium'.[13] This is a troubling trend for digital games in particular. As we have argued elsewhere:

> To play a remediated neomedieval narrative is to doubly reinforce both the narrative structure, and the corresponding tropes – in this case a both western aesthetic and narrative structure built on pop-culture cultural constructs. The effective immediacy of the experience encourages players to view the experience as 'real' and 'representative' because of the replicated and remediated tropes and forms.[14]

This leaves the average layperson and player unable to muster a cogent response to remediated texts and histories. Their intellectual framework for understanding the difference between fact and fiction is ill-suited for the task because the assumptions of their ideas about history are just as mis-constructed as the tropes that inform them. And while the game's use of these remediated histories is perfectly justifiable for the purposes of historical fiction and entertainment, the degree to which audiences fall into the trap of belief is more troubling. Because, as Matthew Kapell and Andrew Elliott would argue:

> When history can be simulated, re-created, subverted, and rewritten on a variety of levels, new questions arise about the relationship between video games and the history they purport to represent, questions that traditional historical approaches cannot properly address.[15]

This is a very real tension that any mediated narrative wrestles with. But we would argue that the reality of this tension does not efface the ability of actual historical analysis to engage and mitigate. This chapter, then, seeks to address the representational complications within *Assassin's Creed* by drawing out the remediated and troped influences within the game that efface historical referents in favour of neomedieval thematics that privilege problematic contemporary narratives.

Considering how to approach this is, it seems to us, a significant role for history and historians in the contemporary moment; 'if everything is historical, then history becomes that which we choose'.[16] And this is the issue. The historical façade of *Assassin's Creed* is not exclusively the fault of the designers. Indeed, they have done due diligence in attempting to craft an engaging piece of historical fiction. The issue is how the broader map of what constitutes history has been redefined by a combination of two factors: (1) the increasing verisimilitude of historical fiction, and (2) a ready willingness to ignore the history of narrative thematics, appropriations, and remediations within this game as a text. To solve this, our argument traces the origin of the *Assassin's Creed* game not from historical and archival texts, but from a chain of remediated fictions. Because remediation is always about calling to mind the thing that came before as a way to validate the newly formed media object, it participates in the replication and reiteration of narrative and thematic tropes that are the hallmark of the genre. These tropes are always grounded in ideological systems that produce them, and as a result carry over into the newly mediated form. In this case, the video game becomes understood as 'history' because an audience mistakes its various tropes as such.

Representational Narratives and *Assassin's Creed*

In brief form, *Assassin's Creed* takes place in the near-future – 2012, six years ahead of the production date of the game. A bartender named Desmond Miles is seized by agents of a pharmaceutical conglomerate named Abstergo Industries and taken to their headquarters in Rome. There, he is attached to a machine called the 'Animus', which is capable of turning the 'Genetic memories' of his ancestors into a virtual reality simulation that he is then forced to explore. The scientist controlling the laboratory, Dr. Vidic, and his assistant, Lucy Stillman, instruct him to relive the life of Altaïr ibn-La'Ahad, one of the most important members of the Assassins Brotherhood during the era of the Third Crusade. Over the course of the game, Desmond experiences Altaïr botch an attack to retrieve a mysterious artefact called the 'Piece of Eden' from the Grand Master of the Knights Templar, Robert de Sablé, then return to his home base of Maysaf just in time to fight off a Crusader assault, and as a result be demoted and assigned a series of missions by his mentor and the leader of the Assassins, Al Mualim, in order to redeem himself. He assassinates nine individuals, Christian and Muslim, and in the process discovers that they all are secretly Templars, trying to find an 'Apple of Eden', another mysterious relic that they believe had mystical powers. Eventually, Altaïr catches Robert de Sablé in King Richard I's camp, exposes his crimes to the king and undertakes a duel to decide the guilty. Robert loses, and tells Altaïr as he lies dying that Al Mualim had also been a Templar and betrayed them to get the Apple himself. Altaïr races back to Maysaf to discover that Al Mualim has mind-controlled the inhabitants by using the Apple. Finally, Altaïr battles Al Mualim, wins, and attempts to destroy the Apple – an attempt that fails and instead shows a map with the location of countless other 'Pieces of Eden' around the world. At this point, Desmond is pulled out of the simulation, and Dr. Vidic reveals that Abstergo is the modern incarnation of the Templars, still looking for the Pieces of Eden. His assistant, Lucy, turns out to be a secret agent of the modern Assassins, and she disappears. Desmond is placed in a secured room, and while he waits for her to return and rescue him, he discovers strange drawing all over the walls which foretell of an apocalyptic event that will wipe out humanity, setting up the rest of the series.

There are numerous problematic ideologies at play within the game, but one of the clearest and most damaging comes via the in-game mechanism that allows the series to function: the 'Animus' and the ability the experience 'genetic memories'. The device, like all science fiction, is designed to enable storytelling through semi-scientific means. And like all good science fiction it has just enough plausible science to back it up conceptually.[17] In this case, the conceptual model for 'genetic memories' is epigenetics, a series of 'alterations in the chemical modification of DNA that do not involve modifying the actual DNA sequence', leaving marks on the DNA sequence that are sometimes described 'the ghosts in our genes' due to their inheritability.[18] As a scientific principle, the study is fascinating:

> Epigenetic information is encrypted in genetic sequences, and includes DNA methylation, histone modifications and small RNA changes (Bonasio et al., 2010). Epigenetic memory is the ability to transfer epigenetic information from one generation to the next. Epigenetic information uses patterns of inheritance, which are not determined by DNA sequence alone and may result in an epigenetic memory, which like genetic memory can be stably inherited and passed onto progeny through meiosis, although epigenetic inheritance mainly defies Mendelian laws.[19]

A 2013 study in mice found that epigenetic memory could include inheriting trauma from parents – in that case, passing on a phobia to a smell like cherry blossoms – that led to the grandchildren of the test subjects avoiding the scent of cherry blossoms.[20] All of this work has incredible possibilities for thinking about environmental factors in the health and development of people and societies over generations – not only legal implications, but ethical implications in environmental justice, intergenerational equity, and equitable access to health care.[21] It also leads to possible future problems – privacy and confidentiality, especially, but also, critically, eugenics:

> The moral imperative to consider the transgenerational effects of environmentally-induced epigenetic changes suggests the following intergenerational genetic and epigenetic principle: Each generation should maintain the quality of the human genome and epigenome and pass it on in no worse condition than the present generation received it. Although such a principle is consonant with intergenerational equity generally and is appealing in the abstract, its application must be carefully circumscribed or it could lead to eugenic policies.[22]

While *Assassin's Creed* does not discuss eugenics, does not extend into the twentieth century or act upon the 'genetic memory' notion beyond the

'Animus', the games requires the notion that blood and genealogy matter in clear, direct, and DNA-related ways. This is not a new issue within medievalist gaming – Amy Kaufman and Cory Grewell wrote on this problem in 'Blood Will Out: Genealogy as Destiny in Medieval(ist) Gaming' in 2012 – but *Assassin's Creed* builds an entire extended universe on the notion of blood genealogy as the key to the survival of the human race.[23] It does not help that the Abstergo operator of the Animus, Dr. Warren Vidic, is a white-haired, white-bearded, white-skinned older man, aided by Lucy, modelled on and voiced by Kristen Bell: white characters operating a machine focused on blood genealogy in order to access secret conspiracies of the past to control the present. Desmond Miles, however, is modelled on a Latino French-Canadian model, chosen by the casting department of Ubisoft who were 'searching for a face with Mediterranean traits to render that person in the time of the Crusades'.[24] The use of genetics and science to dominate humanity – run by the Abstergo-Templars, of course – and to locate key genetic lines to be used to preserve the species is close enough to genetic fascism past and present to be concerning all on its own.[25]

If 'genetic memory' of the right bloodlines is the key to accessing the past, what then of that past? As it is portrayed in *Assassin's Creed*, the medieval Middle East is, in the time of the Third Crusade, in the midst of a model of 'clash of civilizations' between Christianity and Islam in ways that do not flatter either. Visually speaking, the game and, indeed, the entire series are aesthetically rich, constructing a neomedieval vision of the Middle East with detailed cityscapes, architecture, clothing, and weapons, all of the trappings of a popular image of the past – Nicolas Cantin, the pre-production art director and the art director for cinematics, said that:

> [There was] a lot of research on my part about all of those cities at the medieval time, during the Crusade, you know, to make sure we were doing something a little bit more realistic than fantasy. When you work with history, you need to take it a little bit more seriously, I think. And without, you know, making sure that everything is like the history.[26]

The two parts of that statement – doing a lot of research on the aesthetics 'without, you know, making sure that everything is like the history' describes both the appeal and the continuous problem of neomedieval video games. Indeed, other scholars have noted the striking attention to details the game (and its sequels) afford to setting, architecture, and character design.[27] This verisimilitude is key to the persuasive power of the game's ability to represent neomedieval history.

For *Assassin's Creed*, the 'history' that sparked that concept for Patrice Désilets, the creative director, happened when he 'looked around and I stumbled upon a book about secret societies that I read in college. And it was kinda like a little book of all the myths surrounding super-secret societies. And the first story was about the Old Men of the Mountain. About the Assassins'.[28] While the book itself is unidentified, books on secret societies abound. When the development team at Ubisoft Montreal went beyond the concept to doing research, they said that, 'Our main reference was the book *Alamut*, which was about the assassins at the time of the medieval crusade'.[29] And here is where the genesis of the historical framework of the game really falls apart – a combination of conspiracy theories for the idea and a Slovenian novel about the Assassins, written by Vladimir Bartol in Paris in the 1930s and inspired by contemporary events around the rise of fascism and Slovene nationalism.[30] To wit, a work of historical fiction published in the nineteenth century serves as the foundation for 'historical fact'. This is remediation at its most precise.

The novel creates a vision of the 'Assassins' that is, as with almost all portrayals of the group, an Orientalist fantasy of a real group – the Nizari Ismailis, the largest segment of the Ismaili Shi'ite community today, who are, themselves, the second-largest branch of Shia Islam after the Imamiyyah, and are today led by the Aga Khan and based in Lisbon, Portugal.[31] At their foundation, the Nizaris were a product of a schism within the Ismaili movement during a brief civil war in the Fatimid Caliphate of Egypt, just before the start of the twelfth century.[32] Even within their community, they were an embattled minority – and outside of it, they were within hostile territory.

While scattered literary texts of the Nizaris survive, most accounts of the Nizaris come from external sources, almost all of whom were deeply hostile to them. These hostile portrayals fundamentally shape the way the Nizari Ismailis were understood, not only in the Middle Ages but in the nineteenth century and, through those authors, in the modern day.[33] In many ways the Latin sources are kinder to the Nizaris than other Islamic portrayals (usually Sunni in origin), which focused on religious difference.[34] In Europe, stories of Alamut were passed along not through the rich variety of Islamic or Mongol sources, but through the Travels of Marco Polo, the great blockbuster travel fiction of the Middle Ages. His description of 'The Old Man of the Mountain' and Alamut describes it as a paradise garden filled with palaces, fruit trees, wine, music, and a promise on the part of the leader that Muhammad had said that those who obeyed him would enjoy every sexual gratification imaginable.[35] As a result, his subjects would do anything for him, and would kill anyone he asked, happy to die for him because of the promise of that paradise. Marco Polo's account ends with the destruction of Alamut by Hulagu in 1262. This particular account would become the dominant one for nineteenth-century European orientalists, inflaming the imagination and becoming the standard depiction leading up to Bartol's *Alamut*.[36]

Bartol's *Alamut*, then, one of the most important inspirations for the game, is a fictitious work based on orientalist accounts formed by one of the most significant pieces of medieval western travel fantasy. Small wonder, then, that the book forms but one part of a broader orientalist fantasy of the Assassins in the twentieth and early twenty-first centuries. As Mirt Komel has argued,

Bartol's *Alamut* is just one peg of a longer series of re-orientalising the Assassins throughout the latter half of the twentieth century to turn them into the forerunners of modern terrorism, specifically, the later texts get in the twentieth and especially into the twenty-first century, as forerunners of modern Islamic fundamentalism and *jihadi* terrorism.[37] The catch-phrase of Bartol's Assassins, 'nothing is true, everything is permitted', that became a conceptual framework for *Assassin's Creed*, was created as a commentary on Silvestre de Sacy's 1838 essay *Exposé de la Religion des Druzes*, one of a series of texts he wrote based on Marco Polo's conceptions of the Assassins.[38] When Bartol's work was translated into French in 1988, it was promoted as a faithful historical account of eleventh-century Persia but also as a key for understanding Muslim support for their religious leaders, specifically in a post-Iranian Revolution context.[39] It would not be translated into English until 2004, when it was promoted in the post-9/11 world as a fictionalised-but-rational explanation for the behaviour of groups like al-Qaeda.[40] By this point, Bernard Lewis, one of the major figures in popular Middle Eastern history, had devoted the final chapter of his revised 2003 edition of *Assassins: A Radical Sect in Islam* to showing that the Nizari had invented terrorism.[41]

The text of *Alamut*, though, while being used as a window into Islam, is a deeply Western text – an orientalised setting and aesthetic, much like *Assassin's Creed*, mixed with a worldview that is fundamentally Western in philosophy, especially Machiavellian, and focused on the political landscape on 1930s Yugoslavia. *Assassin's Creed* follows this, turning the ostensibly Nizari Ismaili protagonist – the 'Assassin' – into a character that is aesthetically orientalist while simultaneously divorcing the character from religion, culture and any sense of othering.[42] In the game, this is accomplished via the player, coming from a Western perspective; the Animus-driven virtual reality landscape; and the Western philosophical underpinning of the source material for the game combine to take the Assassins from being the orientalised forerunners of modern terrorism into a heroic, westernised protagonist. This ludic framework serves the purposes of reinforcing the familiar tropes of Western cultural frameworks, deepening the neomedieval illusion in their historical veracity.

If the Assassin becomes a by-and-large secular, Western protagonist, what of the villains and historical antagonists of the Syrian Assassins, the Templars? If the problematic nature of *Assassin's Creed* thus far has been a focus on the importance of blood, blood purity, and blood genealogy, combined with a deeply orientalised perspective of the Nizari Ismaili that both exoticises them and removes any aspect of their actual Islamic identity, then the Templar conspiracy theory that underpins the narrative arc forms the final and most damningly problematic aspect of the game. Templar conspiracy theories are, of course, by this point so common in popular culture as to be somewhat laughable. As Umberto Eco wrote, 'The lunatic is all idée fixe, and whatever he comes across confirms his lunacy. You can tell him by the liberties he takes with common sense, by his flashes of inspiration, and by the fact that sooner or later he brings up the Templars'.[43] And it is those Templars – the conspiratorial ones – rather than the actual Templars, who are the antagonists of the game. While the aesthetics and names of the characters in *Assassin's Creed* are based on historical reality, what of the idea of the survival of the Templars past the early fourteenth-century trials and dissolution of the Order, of hidden treasures located under Solomon's Temple, and of a conspiracy of global domination using artefacts of a non-human origin?[44] These are all wrapped up in a web of popular conspiracies that inevitably fall into white supremacist and far-right ideological traps.

There are enough Templar conspiracies that we can only look at three here, but those are enough to show where the game is indulging in them. First, there is the notion of the hidden Templars being part of some kind of shadow government. This is the theory Umberto Eco plays with in *Foucault's Pendulum,* but comes out of the French Revolution, originally. The illegitimate son of Louis XV, Charles-Louis Cadet de Gassicourt, was a lawyer, pharmacist, and writer who, in 1791, wrote a text entitled 'The Tomb of Jacques de Molay, or the Secret History and Summary of the Ancient and Modern Initiates of the Templars, Freemasons and Illuminati', which claimed that the French Revolution was the final step of an almost 500-year-old revenge plot by the surviving Templars.[45] By 1797, two other books were published by John Robinson, a Scotsman, and Abbé Augustin Barruel, a French refugee of the revolution, building a larger set of conspiracies of French Freemasons, the Bavarian Illuminati, and French *philosophes* as secretly masterminding the Revolution – and, in the case of Barruel, linking these groups back to a series of older groups, including the Templars.[46] From these feeble but influential foundations, the notion of the survival of the Knights Templar and their links to Freemasonry, and, via the conspiracy theories around Freemasons, to a wide range of shadow government conspiracies was born.[47]

The second conspiracy is the notion of a Templar discovery of the New World, usually associated with the so-called 'Oak Island Mystery', but problematic not only for the notions of a hidden Templar treasure (to be discussed next) but because of white nationalist ideologies wrapped up in pre-Columbian European contacts with the Americas. There is, of course, absolutely no evidence of this happening, and yet conspiracies continue based on fictitious documents called the *Zeno Narrative* about an end of the fourteenth-century transatlantic voyage by the Earl of Orkney, Henry Saint-Clair, in partnership with a Venetian merchant family called the Zenos.[48] The Saint-Clair family had also been claimed as descendants of the Knights Templar, builders of Rosslyn Chapel and a whole host of other conspiracies involving the Templars previously.[49] Much like modern misusage of Vinland, however, the claims to pre-Columbian European settlement in the Americas have been used by the far-right to bolster white supremacist narratives of ownership over North America.[50] The final bit of this conspiracy, the idea that a Templar fleet made it to Oak Island off the coast of Nova Scotia and buried a secret treasure in the so-called 'money pit', has, unfortunately, lived on and is now the subject of a History Channel television series.[51] The 1999 book *The Lost Treasures of the Knights Templar: Solving the Oak Island Mystery* expanded the idea, and the placing of *Assassin's Creed III* and *IV*[52] in North America, continuing the Templar-conspiracy-through-time narrative, only makes those links more problematic.[53]

The Oak Island conspiracy gives way to the final, and most problematic, part of the Templar conspiracy theories linked to *Assassin's Creed*: the notion of the hidden treasure of the Templars and, specifically, the idea that it is an artefact of exceptional power. The Shroud of Turin has in the past been connected to this by conspiracy theorists – Ian Wilson, for example, claimed in his 1979 *The Turin Shroud: The Burial Cloth of Jesus Christ?* that the Templars may have found Jesus' preserved head and used the shroud to carry it.[54] The 'Priory of Sion' conspiracies best known from Dan Brown's *The Da Vinci Code* and its main conspiracy theory forefather, Michael Baigent, Richard Leigh and Henry Lincoln's *The Holy Blood and the Holy Grail,* advance the idea of a secret order which created the Knights Templar as part of a two millennia-long guarding of the descendants of Jesus and Mary Magdalene.[55] The Templars in *Assassin's Creed*, though, are seeking a physical object of immense power: a relic of a previous civilisation. The 'Apples of Eden', as the game refers to them, are ancient artefacts of a civilisation that predates humanity, which can be used to effectively mind-control human beings. Circulating throughout history, these objects are used by significant people across time to enact pivotal social changes. The game's narrative depicts the Templar order seeking to obtain and use these objects to enact social control for what they believe is the greater good.

This story is the best kind of entertainment fiction, but it is a remediated concept. In this case, the conspiracy theory forefather of this notion is not a relatively harmless conspiracy, but a German writer named Otto Rahn, who published two books in the 1930s on the Holy Grail, the Cathars, and the Knights Templar: *Kreuzzug gegen den Gral* in 1933 and *Luzifers Hofgesind* in 1937.[56] These two texts posited that the German epic *Parzival* was a historical text, and that the Cathar (Templars) stronghold of Montségur was the secret repository of the Holy Grail.[57] The idea of the Templars carrying off a secret relic from the Holy Land and hiding it would be taken off by other, later conspiracies – but the concept was appealing in the 1930s to Heinrich Himmler, who had Otto Rahn inducted into the SS to pursue his research in 1935.[58] Rahn would die in 1939 of exposure. The groups that would be early backers of the Nazis, especially those with occult interests, would continue to be interested in his work and at least one branch of them, organised by Adolf Josef Lanz, would construct a 'Order of the New Templars' connecting the same types of Parsifal-Grail interests Rahn would later develop for southern France with genealogical and heraldic research towards building an Aryan aristocratic order whose height of activities was between 1925 and 1935, after which it fizzled out.[59] Because *Assassin's Creed* so deftly remediates historical artifice with fictional narratives, it is a vehicle that reinforces all Templar/Grail mythos by calling them all to memory. Likewise, because *Assassin's Creed* works in these remediated spaces, it equally calls to mind the multiple ideological and rhetorical affordances associated with Templar/Grail mythos.

These ideologies – blood genealogy, Templar conspiracies, violent orientalised Islam without building a player-connection – are not in and of themselves unique. Indeed, one of the most problematic parts of the neomedieval video game landscape is how widespread ethnonationalist ideologies are throughout modern games. *Assassin's Creed*, however, came out in 2007, the year before Richard Spencer coined the term 'Alternative Right'.[60] And on 22 July 2011, Anders Behring Breivik killed 76 people in Norway in a far-right terrorist attack, after issuing a long compendium of texts entitled *2083: A European Declaration of Independence* proclaiming himself a member of the New Knights Templar and blaming Islam and feminism for the decline of European culture that led to his attack. The alt-right have, since then, adopted neomedieval language, garb, and faux-histories, and further far-right terrorists have gravitated to the language of neo-crusading that Breivik adopted. Video games do not, of course, cause people to engage in mass murder, but the neomedieval tropes within *Assassin's Creed* provided fertile ground for the alt-right to engage in false historical arguments to bolster far-right aims, something that continued to develop through GamerGate and the expansion of 4chan far-right activity.[61]

Historical Ethos and the Contemporary Moment

The most difficult part of this work is attempting to chart some sense of implications for the future. We are well beyond simple declarations on whether *Assassin's Creed* is 'good' or 'bad'. Any such conclusion would be both disingenuous and sloppy. That fact that it requires such a detailed analysis is testament to both its success as a neomedieval remediation, and its value as an entertainment artefact. It successfully spawned a media franchise that has lasted more than a decade and continues to capture the imagination. In 2020, Ubisoft released *Assassin's Creed: Valhalla*, which relocated the story of the Assassins into Nordic culture. This cultural shift already heralds concerns given the frequent overlap between neomedieval Nordicity and the cultural capital of ethno-nationalists.[62] Indeed, work linking the far-right's appropriation of these tropes is well under way.[63] Games like *Assassin's Creed* serve to reinforce the historical fictions at the expense of historical inquiry by presenting remediated tropes as monolithic; they construct neomedieval realities by mapping contemporary assumptions, ideas, and values onto historical frameworks. Built on the skeletal bones of actual historical past, these fictions produce narrative homunculi by fleshing out the complexity of actual history on a much smaller scale. This makes fertile ground for audiences to skirt the more complicated goal of counterfactual play, instead opting to grow more problematic transmedia assumptions from this contemporary remediated message. We should also remember though, that they do not pretend to be history. While not all games are exclusively grounded as entertainment media, *Assassin's Creed* games certainly are. It is precisely that intersection that makes them easily remediated, because the goal is often aligned with the player's desire. Ubisoft executives have directly been asked if there are perspectives they would refuse to indulge or engage with; their response, as quoted in *Variety Magazine*, was:

> We believe that ultimately, in the future, players should be able to go in the game world, have as many different experiences as they want, experience as many different political views as they want, as many religions as they want […] as many different fantasies as they want.[64]

What then is the role of history in this moment? This project comes at the intersection of two writers – one a crusades historian and the other a rhetorician – who believe that only through the careful, continued, and public challenging of neomedieval remediations can such moves be resisted. The entertainment value of such fictions is undeniable. We, along with countless others, enjoy them greatly, but we cannot allow our fictions to become the strict lens through which we read our history. Otherwise, we risk losing sight of the moral and cultural complexity of the real world in favour of the convenient fictions we use to self-justify our existing ontologies.

Notes

1 'Ubisoft Announces Outstanding Sales Performance for *Assassin's Creed*™ and Raises Guidance for Fiscal 2007–08', 2007 <https://web.archive.org/web/20071218091159/http://www.ubi.com/US/News/Info.aspx?nId=5017> [accessed 29 November 2019].

2 Christine Fisher, '"*Assassin's Creed* Symphony" Concerts Will Also Feature Holograms', *engadget*, 9 April 2019 <https://www.engadget.com/2019/04/09/assassins-creed-symphony-trailer/> [accessed 29 November 2019].

3 J. Clement, 'Lifetime Unit Sales Generated by the Assassin's Creed Series Worldwide as of September 2022', *Statista*, 2 December 2022 <https://www.statista.com/statistics/1276750/assassins-creed-lifetime-unit-sales/> [accessed 29 December 2023].

4 Tom Apperley, 'Modding the Historians' Code: Historical Verisimilitude and the Counterfactual Imagination', in *Playing with the Past: Digital Games and the Simulation of History,* ed. Matthew Wilhelm Kapell and Andrew B.R. Elliott (New York, 2013), p. 184.

5 Matthew Wilhelm Kapell and Andrew B.R Elliott, 'Introduction: To Build a Past that Will "Stand the Test of Time" – Discovering Historical Facts, Assembling Historical Narratives', in *Playing with the Past*, p. 17.

6 Ibid, p. 5.

7 Adam Chapman, *Digital Games as History: How Video Games Represent the Past and Offer Access to Historical Practice* (New York, 2016), pp. 177–9.
8 Frank Bosman, ‘Nothing Is True, Everything Is Permitted: The Portrayal of the Nizari Isma’ilis in the *Assassin’s Creed* Game Series’, *Heidelberg Journal of Religions on the Internet*, 10 (2016), pp. 6–26.
9 Bosman, ‘Nothing Is True, Everything Is Permitted .
10 Ubisoft Montreal, *Assassin’s Creed*, 2007.
11 Beth A. Dillon, ‘Signifying the West: Colonialist Design in *Age of Empires III: The WarChiefs*’, *Eludamos - Journal for Computer Game Culture*, 2 (2008), pp. 129–44; Marku Eskellinan, ‘Towards Computer Game Studies’, in *First Person: New Media as Story, Performance, and Game*, ed. Noah Wardrip-Fruin and Pat Harrigan (Cambridge, MA, 2004), p. 331; Adrienne Shaw, ‘The Tyranny of Realism: Historical Accuracy and Politics of Representation in *Assassin’s Creed III*’, *Loading... The Journal of the Canadian Game Studies Association*, 9 (2014), pp. 4–24; Martin Lorber and Felix Zimmerman, eds, *History in Games: Contingencies of an Authentic Past* (New York, 2020).
12 Jean Baudrillard, ‘The Order of Simulacra’, trans. Iain Hamilton Grant, in *Symbolic Exchange and Death* (London, 1993), p. 74.
13 Astrid Erll and Ann Rigney, *Mediation, Remediation, and the Dynamics of Cultural Memory* (New York, 2009), p. 4.
14 Joshua Call and Thomas Lecaque, ‘From Hero to Zero: Nationalistic Narratives and the Dogma of Being Dragonborn’, in *Being Dragonborn: Critical Essays on The Elder Scrolls V: Skyrim*, ed. Mike Piero and Marc A. Ouellette (Jefferson, NC, 2021), pp. 14–27.
15 Kapell and Elliott, ‘Introduction’, p. 2.
16 Paul Veyne, *Comment on ecrit l’histoire*, trans. Elliott and Kapell, in ‘Introduction’, p. 5.
17 Sebastian Alvarado, ‘The Science Fact Animating *Assassin’s Creed*’s Animus’, *Kotaku*, 11 April 2012 <https://kotaku.com/the-science-fact-animating-assassins-creeds-animus-5901160> [accessed 29 November 2019].
18 Mark A. Rothstein, Yu Cai and Gary E. Marchant, ‘The Ghost in Our Genes: Legal and Ethical Implications of Epigenetics’, *Health Matrix Clevel*, 19 (2009), pp. 1–62 <https://www.ncbi.nlm.nih.gov/pmc/articles/PMC3034450/> [accessed 2 June 2023].
19 Zoe Migicovsky and Igor Kovalchuk, ‘Epigenetic Memory in Mammals’, *Frontiers in Genetics*, 2 (2011), pp. 1–7.
20 Brian G. Dias and Kerry J. Ressler, ‘Parental Olfactory Experience Influences Behavior and Neural Structure in Subsequent Generations’, *Nature Neuroscience*, 17 (2014), pp. 89–96.
21 Rothstein, Cai and Marchant, ‘Ghost in Our Genes’.
22 Rothstein, Cai and Marchant, ‘Ghost in Our Genes’. See also Luca Chiapperino, ‘Epigenetics: Ethics, Politics, Biosociality’, *British Medical Bulletin*, 128 (2018), pp. 49–60, esp. p. 55, where he briefly discusses the concerns around ‘epi-eugenics’, and E.T. Juengst, J.R. Fishman, M.L. McGowan and R.A. Settersten Jr., ‘Serving Epigenetics Before Its Time’, *Trends in Genetics*, 30 (2014), pp. 427–9, which coined the term epi-eugenics.
23 Amy S. Kaufman and Cory Grewell, ‘Blood Will Out: Genealogy as Destiny in Medieval(ist) Gaming’, in *Neomedievalism in the Media: Essays on Film, Television, and Electronic Games*, ed. Carol L. Robinson and Pamela Clements (Lewiston, 2012).
24 ‘La production cherchait un visage aux traits méditerranéens pour rendre ce personnage du temps des Croisades’. Sophie Bernard, ‘[*Assassin’s Creed*] Francisco Randez prête son visage à Altaïr’, *Lien Multimédia*, 23 November 2007 <http://www.lien-multimedia.com/article.php3?id_article=13885> [accessed 29 November 2019].

The idea of 'Mediterraneans' as a race, while certainly not the intention of the casting call, has a problematic history since 1899, when William Z. Ripley divided Europeans into 'Tuetons', 'Alpines', and 'Mediterraneans', as one of the early influential proponents of 'race science'. See Adam Serwer, 'White Nationalisms' Deep American Roots', *The Atlantic*, April 2019 <https://www.theatlantic.com/magazine/archive/2019/04/adam-serwer-madison-grant-white-nationalism/583258/> [accessed 29 November 2019].

25 For 'genetic fascism' as a term, see Eric B. Brown, 'The Dilemmas of German Bioethics', *The New Atlantis*, 5 (2004), p. 38.

26 Richard Moss, '*Assassin's Creed*: An Oral History', *Polygon*, 3 October 2019 <https://www.polygon.com/features/2018/10/3/17924770/assassins-creed-an-oral-history-patrice-desilets> [accessed 29 November 2019].

27 Jonathan Westin and Ragnar Hedlund, 'Polychronia – Negotiating the Popular Representation of a Common Past in *Assassin's Creed*', *Journal of Gaming and Virtual Worlds*, 8 (2016), pp. 3–20; Shaw, 'Tyranny of Realism'; Bosman, 'Nothing Is True'.

28 Richard Moss, '*Assassin's Creed*: An Oral History', *Polygon*, 3 October 2019 <https://www.polygon.com/features/2018/10/3/17924770/assassins-creed-an-oral-history-patrice-desilets> [accessed 29 November 2019].

29 Ibid. That quote is disputed later in the oral history, where Patrice Désiltets says that, 'I re-read a bunch of stuff. I think it was the second month or third month I read *Alamut*, the book that people think was the starting point – but it wasn't. We were already in it. And it's part of the book about who were the assassins. It's just this novel written by like a Slovenian in the 1930s and you should read it. I guess this is where I took the idea of – like the master and the disciple relationship is really strong in *Alamut*. And so that was where the Al Mualim and Altaïr relationship came from'.

30 See the extensive essays by Miran Hladnik on Bartol and *Alamut* on his website: Miram Hladnik, 'Alamut in slovenski literarni ponos', November 2004 <http://www.ijs.si/lit/alamut_radio.html>; 'Vendarle tudi makiavelistični roman?', November 2004 <http://www.ijs.si/lit/alamut4.html>; 'Razmerje med Bartolovo kratko in dolgo prozo (Al Araf in Alamut)', 15 September 2007 <http://www.ijs.si/lit/alamut5.html> [all accessed 29 November 2019]. See also the introduction by Michael Biggins in the English language translation of *Alamut*; Vladimir Bartol, *Alamut*, trans. Michael Biggins (Berkeley, 2007).

31 'Seat of Ismaili Imamat', Islamic Publications Limited, 2018 <https://ismaili.imamat/#seat-of-imam> [accessed 2 June 2023].

32 For one quick overview of how the Nizari relate to the 'Assassins' in *Assassin's Creed*, see Mohammad Ballan, 'The Nizari Isma'ili Assassins: The Story behind Ubisoft's "*Assassin's Creed*"', *Ballandalus* (blog), 8 August 2012 <https://ballandalus.wordpress.com/2012/08/08/the-nizari-ismaili-assassins-the-story-behind-ubisofts-assassins-creed-2/> [accessed 29 November 2019]. For the medieval history of the Nizaris, see Farhad Daftary, *Ismailis in Medieval Muslim Societies* (London, 2005), pp. 109–10, and Michael Brett, *The Fatimid Empire* (Edinburgh, 2017), pp. 228–32.

33 The most important chronicle source is William of Tyre, *Chronicon*, ed. Robert B.C. Huygens (Turnhout, 1986), 20:29–32. See Bernard Hamilton, 'The Templars, the Syrian Assassins and King Amalric of Jerusalem', in *The Hospitallers, the Mediterranean and Europe: Festschrift for Anthony Luttrell*, ed. Karl Borchardt, Nikolas Jaspert and Helen J. Nicholson (Aldershot, 2007), pp. 13–24; Peter W. Edbury, 'The Old French William of Tyre, the Templars and the Assassin Envoy', in *The Hospitallers, the Mediterranean and Europe: Festschrift for Anthony Luttrell*, ed. Karl Borchardt, Nikolas Jaspert and Helen J. Nicholson (Aldershot: Ashgate, 2007), pp. 25–39; Philip Handyside, 'The Old French Translation of William of

Tyre' (unpublished PhD thesis, Cardiff University, 2012), pp. 106–7 for the spread of William of Tyre's version.

34 See Bogdan Smarandache, 'The Franks and the Nizari Isma'ilis in the Early Crusade Period', *Al-Masaq*, 24 (2012), pp. 221–4 for a discussion of the source issues for twelfth-century perceptions of the Nizaris, and Natasha Shahid, 'Sectarianist Writings in Islam: Prejudice against the Hashashin in 12th and 13th Century Muslim Historiography', *International Journal of Arts & Sciences*, 9 (2016), pp. 437–48 for a look at their negative portrayal in five well-known Islamic sources. See Shafique N. Virani, *The Ismailis in the Middle Ages: A History of Survival, a Search for Salvation* (Oxford, 2007), for a discussion of the Nizaris in Persia after the Mongol invasion, and especially the destruction of primary Nizari sources.

35 Marco Polo, *Travels of Marco Polo* (London, 1914), Ch. 22, pp. 73–7.

36 Jeffrey Kaplan, 'Nothing Is True, Everything Is Permitted: Premodern Religious Terrorism', *Terrorism and Political Violence*, 31 (2019), pp. 1076–80 discusses the Nizari; Bernard Lewis, 'The Sources for the History of the Syrian Assassins', *Speculum*, 27 (1952), pp. 475–89 laid out many of the early modern and nineteenth-century Orientalist sources for the depiction of the Nizari as the 'Assassins'; and Geraldine Heng, 'Sex, Lies, and Paradise: The Assassins, Prester John, and the Fabulation of Civilizational Identities', *Differences: A Journal of Feminist Cultural Studies*, 25 (2012), pp. 1–31 looks specifically at the portrayal of the 'Assassins' in Marco Polo's *Travels* and John Mandeville's *Travels*.

37 Mirt Komel, 'Re-orientalizing the Assassins in Western Historical-Fiction Literature Orientalism and Self-Orientalism in Bartol's *Alamut*, Tarr's *Alamut*, Boschert's *Assassins of Alamut* and Oden's *Lion of Cairo*', *European Journal of Cultural Studies*, 17 (2014), pp. 525–48.

38 Komel, 'Re-orientalizing', p. 531; Moss, 'An Oral History'; Antoine Isaac Silvestre de Sacy, *Exposé de la religion des druzes, tiré des livres religieux de cette secte, et précédé d'une introduction et de la Vie du khalife Hakem-biamr-Allah* (Paris, 1838); Gustav Flügel, *Die Geschichte Der Araber Bis Auf Den Sturz Des Chalifats Von Bagdad* (Dresden, 1864), p. 251.

39 Komel, 'Re-orientalizing', p. 532.

40 Komel, 'Re-orientalizing', p. 533.

41 Bernard Lewis, *The Assassins: A Radical Sect in Islam* (London, 2003).

42 Mirt Komel, 'Orientalism in *Assassin's Creed:* Self-Orientalizing the Assassins from Forerunners of Modern Terrorism into Occidentalized Heroes', *Teorija in Praksa*, 51 (2014), pp. 72–90.

43 Umberto Eco, *Foucault's Pendulum*, trans. William Weaver (Orlando, 1989), p. 65.

44 For the actual Templars, see Helen J. Nicholson's extensive work on the Templars, including *The Everyday Life of the Templars: The Knights Templar at Home* (Stroud, 2017).

45 Charles-Louis Cadet de Gassicourt, *Le tombeau de Jacques Molai ou Historie secrete et abrégée des initiés, anciens et modernes, des Templiers, franc-maçons, illumines, etc.* (Paris, 1791).

46 John Robinson, *Proofs of a Conspiracy against all the Religions and Governments of Europe, Carried on in the Secret Meetings of Free Masons, Illuminati, and Reading Societies*, 3rd edn (Philadelphia, 1798); L'Abbé Barruel, *Mémoires pour server a l'Histoire du Jacobinisme*, 5 vols. (Hamburg, 1798).

47 John J. Robinson, *Dungeon, Fire and Sword: The Knights Templar in the Crusades* (New York, 1992), ends with a brief discussion of how the Freemasons kept the Templar legacy alive despite lack of clear links between the two.

48 In the nineteenth century, this was taken surprisingly seriously – see *The Voyages of the Venetian brothers Nicolò & Antonio Zeno, to the Northern Seas in the XIVth century*, trans. and ed. With notes and introduction Richard Henry Major (London, 1873) and the Zeno Narrative's biggest proponent, Frederick W. Lucas, *The Annals*

of the Voyages of the Brothers Nicolo and Antonio Zeno in the North Atlantic (London, 1898).

49 These are the kinds of discussions that flow through a variety of older webpages and blogs; for a summary, see Christopher Hodapp and Alice von Kannon, *The Templar Code for Dummies* (Hoboken, NJ, 2007). For major conspiracy theory writings on the Templar-in-America notion, see Tim Wallace-Murphy and Marilyn Hopkins, *Templars in America: From the Crusades to the New World* (New York, 2004) and Ernesto Frers, *The Templar Pirates: The Secret Alliance to Build the New Jerusalem*, trans. Ariel Godwin (Rochester, VT, 2005). Needless to say, neither is a scholarly work and should be treated as the conspiracy theories they are.

50 See David Perry, 'White supremacists love Vikings. But they've got history all wrong', *The Washington Post*, 31 May 2017 <https://www.washingtonpost.com/posteverything/wp/2017/05/31/white-supremacists-love-vikings-but-theyve-got-history-all-wrong/>; Dorothy Kim, 'White SUPREMACISTS Have Weaponized an Imaginary Viking Past. It's Time to Reclaim the Real History', *Time,* 15 April 2019 <https://time.com/5569399/viking-history-white-nationalists/> [both accessed 29 November 2019]; Sverrir Jakobsson, 'Vinland and Wishful Thinking Medieval and Modern Fantasies', *Canadian Journal of History/Annales canadiennes d'histoire*, 47 (2012), pp. 493–514.

51 'The Curse of Oak Island', 2014–present. At the time of publication, the show was in season 11.

52 While *Assassin's Creed IV: Black Flag* is more specifically located in the Caribbean, it continues the freedom vs. control narrative of the Assassin/Templar dynamic by making its protagonist Edward Kenway the ancestor to the protagonist and antagonist of *Assassin's Creed III*. This serves to reinforce the blood genealogy narrative.

53 Steven Sora, *The Lost Treasures of the Knights Templar: Solving the Oak Island Mystery* (Rochester, VT, 1999).

54 Ian Wilson, *The Turin Shroud: The Burial Cloth of Jesus Christ?* (New York, 1979); Hodapp and Kannon, *The Templar Code for Dummies*, 171. Wilson also wrote a pre-Columbian European contact conspiracy book, *The Columbus Myth: Did Men of Bristol Reach America Before Columbus?* (New York, 1992).

55 Dan Brown, *The Da Vinci Code* (New York, 2003) drew inspiration most directly from Lynn Picknett and Clive Prince, *The Templar Revelation: Secret Guardians of the True Identity of Christ* (London, 1997). Michael Baigent, Richard Leigh and Henry Lincoln's *The Holy Blood and the Holy Grail* (London, 1982) is the big proponent of this conspiracy – and again, the focus on bloodline is worth noting.

56 Otto Rahn, *Kreuzzug gegen den Gral. Die Geschichte der Albigenser* (Freiburg, 1933); *Luzifers Hofgesind, eine Reise zu Europas guten Geistern* (Berlin, 1937).

57 Otto Rahn, *Crusade against the Grail: The Struggle between the Cathars, the Templars, and the Church of Rome* (Rochester, VT, 2006), p. 104.

58 Nicolas Goodricke Clark, *The Occult Roots of Nazism: Secret Aryan Cults and their Influence on Nazi Ideology* (London, 2004), p. 189.

59 Clark, *The Occult Roots of Nazism*, pp. 101–22.

60 Matthew N. Lyons, 'Ctrl-Alt-Delete: The Origins and Ideology of the Alternative Right', *Political Research Associates*, 20 January 2017 <https://www.politicalresearch.org/2017/01/20/ctrl-alt-delete-report-on-the-alternative-right#toc-executive-summary> [accessed 29 November 2019].

61 Caitlin Dewey, 'Absolutely Everything You Need to Know to Understand 4chan, the Internet's Own Bogeyman', *The Washington Post*, 25 September 2014 <https://www.washingtonpost.com/news/the-intersect/wp/2014/09/25/absolutely-everything-you-need-to-know-to-understand-4chan-the-internets-own-bogeyman/>; Caitlin Dewey, 'The only guide to Gamergate you will ever need to read', *The Washington Post,* 14 October 2014 <https://www.washingtonpost.com/news/

the-intersect/wp/2014/10/14/the-only-guide-to-gamergate-you-will-ever-need-to-read/> [both accessed 28 November 2020].

62 Call and Lecaque, 'From Hero to Zero'.

63 Pam Nilan 'The Warrior Myth and Other Fantasies', in *Young People and the Far Right* (Palgrave Macmillan Singapore, 2021).

64 Gera, Emily, 'Ubisoft: Our Games May Avoid Political Messages but Are Not Apolitical', *Variety*, 8 June 2019 <https://variety.com/2019/gaming/news/ubisoft-games-politics-1203236706/> [accessed 16 January 2024].

Bibliography

Primary

Barruel, L'Abbé. *Mémoires pour server a l'Histoire du Jacobinisme*. Five volumes. Hamburg: P. Fauche, Libraire, 1798.

Baigent, Michael, Leigh, Richard and Lincoln, Henry. *The Holy Blood and the Holy Grail*. London: Jonathan Cape, 1982.

Bartol, Vladimir. *Alamut*, trans. Michael Biggins. Berkeley, CA: North Atlantic Books, 2007.

Eco, Umberto. *Foucault's Pendulum*, trans. William Weaver. Orlando, FL: Harcourt, 1989.

Flügel, Gustav. *Die Geschichte der Araber bis auf den Sturz des Chalifats von Bagdad*. Dresden: Kessinger Publishing, 1864.

de Gassicourt, Charles-Louis Cadet. *Le tombeau de Jacques Molai ou Historie secrete et abrégée des initiés, anciens et modernes, des Templiers, franc-maçons, illumines, etc*. Paris: Victor Desenne, imprimeur-libraire, 1791.

Lucas, Frederick W. *The Annals of the Voyages of the Brothers Nicolo and Antonio Zeno in the North Atlantic of the Fourteenth Century and the Claim Founded Thereon to a Venetian Discovery of America, a Criticism and an Indictment*. London: Henry Stevens Son and Stiles, 1898.

Marco Polo. *Travels of Marco Polo*. London: J.M. Dent and Sons, 1914.

Rahn, Otto. *Kreuzzug gegen den Gral. Die Geschichte der Albigenser*. Freiburg: Urban-Verlag, 1933.

Rahn, Otto. *Crusade against the Grail: The Struggle between the Cathars, the Templars, and the Church of Rome*. Rochester, VT: Inner Traditions, 2006.

Rahn, Otto. *Luzifers Hofgesind, eine Reise zu Europas guten Geistern*. Berlin and Leipzig: Schwarzhäupter-Verlag, 1937.

Robinson, John. *Proofs of a Conspiracy against all the Religions and Governments of Europe, Carried on in the Secret Meetings of Free Masons, Illuminati, and Reading Societies*, 3rd edn. Philadelphia, PA: T. Dobson, 1798.

Robinson, John J. *Dungeon, Fire and Sword: The Knights Templar in the Crusades*. New York: M. Evans and Company, Inc, 1992.

de Sacy, Antoine Isaac Silvestre. *Exposé de la religion des druzes, tiré des livres religieux de cette secte, et précédé d'une introduction et de la Vie du khalife Hakem-biamr-Allah*. Paris: Imprimerie royale, 1838.

'Seat of Ismaili Imamat'. Islamic Publications Limited, 2018. https://ismaili.imamat/#seat-of-imam.

Ubisoft Montreal. *Assassin's Creed*. Ubisoft, 2007.

The Voyages of the Venetian brothers Nicolò & Antonio Zeno, to the Northern Seas in the XIVth Century, Comprising the Latest Known Accounts of the Lost Colony of Greenland and of the Northmen in America before Columbus, ed. and trans. Richard Henry Major. London: Hakluyt Society, 1873.

William of Tyre. *Chronicon*, ed. Robert B.C. Huygens. Five volumes. Turnhout: Brepols, 1986.

Secondary

Alvarado, Sebastian. 'The Science Fact Animating *Assassin's Creed*'s Animus'. *Kotaku*, 11 April 2012. https://kotaku.com/the-science-fact-animating-assassins-creeds-animus-5901160.

Apperley, Tom. 'Modding the Historians' Code: Historical Verisimilitude and the Counterfactual Imagination'. In *Playing with the Past: Digital Games and the Simulation of History*, ed. Matthew Wilhelm Kapell and Andrew B.R. Elliott. New York: Bloomsbury, 2013, pp. 185–98.

Ballan, Mohammad. 'The Nizari Isma'ili Assassins: The Story behind Ubisoft's "*Assassin's Creed*"'. *Ballandalus* (blog), 8 August 2012. https://ballandalus.wordpress.com/2012/08/08/the-nizari-ismaili-assassins-the-story-behind-ubisofts-assassins-creed-2/.

Baudrillard, Jean. *Symbolic Exchange and Death*, trans. Iain Hamilton Grant. London: Sage, 1993.

Bernard, Sophie. '[*Assassin's Creed*] Francisco Randez prête son visage à Altaïr'. *Lien Multimédia*, 23 November 2007. http://www.lienmultimedia.com/article.php3?id_article=13885.

Bosman, Frank. 'Nothing Is True, Everything Is Permitted: The portrayal of the Nizari Isma'ilis in the *Assassin's Creed* game series'. *Heidelberg Journal of Religions on the Internet* 10 (2016), pp. 6–26.

Brett, Michael. *The Fatimid Empire*. Edinburgh: Edinburgh University Press, 2017.

Brown, Dan. *The Da Vinci Code*. New York: Doubleday, 2003.

Brown, Eric B. 'The Dilemmas of German Bioethics'. *The New Atlantis* 5 (2004), pp. 37–53.

Call, Joshua and Lecaque, Thomas. 'From Hero to Zero: Nationalistic Narratives and the Dogma of Being Dragonborn'. In *Being Dragonborn: Critical Essays on the Elder Scrolls V: Skyrim*, ed. Mike Piero and Marc A. Ouellette. Jefferson, NC: McFarland Publishing, 2021, pp. 14–27.

Chapman, Adam. *Digital Games as History: How Video Games Represent the Past and Offer Access to Historical Practice*. New York: Taylor and Francis, 2016.

Chiapperino, Luca. 'Epigenetics: Ethics, Politics, Biosociality'. *British Medical Bulletin* 128 (2018), pp. 49–60.

Clark, Nicolas Goodricke. *The Occult Roots of Nazism: Secret Aryan Cults and their Influence on Nazi Ideology*. London: Tauris Parke Paperbacks, 2004.

Daftary, Farhad. *Ismailis in Medieval Muslim Societies*. London: I.B. Tauris Publishers, 2005.

Dewey, Caitlin. 'Absolutely Everything You Need to Know to Understand 4chan, the Internet's Own Bogeyman'. *The Washington Post*, 25 September 2014. https://www.washingtonpost.com/news/the-intersect/wp/2014/09/25/absolutely-everything-you-need-to-know-to-understand-4chan-the-internets-own-bogeyman/.

Dewey, Caitlin. 'The Only Guide to Gamergate You Will Ever Need to Read'. *The Washington Post*, 14 October 2014. https://www.washingtonpost.com/news/the-intersect/wp/2014/10/14/the-only-guide-to-gamergate-you-will-ever-need-to-read/.

Dias, Brian G. and Ressler, Kerry J. 'Parental Olfactory Experience Influences Behavior and Neural Structure in Subsequent Generations'. *Nature Neuroscience* 17 (2014), pp. 89–96.

Dillon, Beth A. 'Signifying the West: Colonialist Design in *Age of Empires III: The WarChiefs*'. *Eludamos – Journal for Computer Game Culture* 2 (2008), pp. 129–44.

Edbury, Peter W. 'The Old French William of Tyre, the Templars and the Assassin Envoy'. In *The Hospitallers, the Mediterranean and Europe: Festschrift for Anthony Luttrell*, ed. Karl Borchardt, Nikolas Jaspert and Helen J. Nicholson. Aldershot: Ashgate, 2007, pp. 25–39.

Erll, Astrid and Rigney, Ann. *Mediation, Remediation, and the Dynamics of Cultural Memory*. New York: Walter de Gruyter, 2009.

Eskellinan, Marku. 'Towards Computer Game Studies'. In *First Person: New Media as Story, Performance, and Game*, ed. Noah Wardrip-Fruin and Pat Harrigan. Cambridge: MIT, 2004, pp. 36–44.

Fisher, Christine. '"*Assassin's Creed* Symphony" Concerts Will also Feature Holograms'. *Engadget*, 9 April 2019. https://www.engadget.com/2019/04/09/assassins-creed-symphony-trailer/.

Frers, Ernesto. *The Templar Pirates: The Secret Alliance to Build the New Jerusalem*, trans. Ariel Godwin. Rochester, Vermont: Destiny Books, 2005.

Gera, Emily, 'Ubisoft: Our Games may Avoid Political Messages but Are Not Apolitical'. *Variety*, 8 June 2019. https://variety.com/2019/gaming/news/ubisoft-games-politics-1203236706/.

Hamilton, Bernard. 'The Templars, the Syrian Assassins and King Amalric of Jerusalem'. In *The Hospitallers, the Mediterranean and Europe: Festschrift for Anthony Luttrell*, ed. Karl Borchardt, Nikolas Jaspert and Helen J. Nicholson. Aldershot: Ashgate, 2007, pp. 13–24.

Handyside, Philip. 'The Old French Translation of William of Tyre'. PhD Dissertation, Cardiff University, 2012.

Heng, Geraldine. 'Sex, Lies, and Paradise: The Assassins, Prester John, and the Fabulation of Civilizational Identities'. *Differences: A Journal of Feminist Cultural Studies* 25 (2012), pp. 1–31.

Hladnik, Miram. 'Alamut in slovenski literarni ponos', November 2004. http://www.ijs.si/lit/alamut_radio.html.

Hladnik, Miram. 'Razmerje med Bartolovo kratko in dolgo prozo (Al Araf in Alamut)', 15 September 2007. http://www.ijs.si/lit/alamut5.html.

Hladnik, Miram. 'Vendarle tudi makiavelistični roman?' November 2004. http://www.ijs.si/lit/alamut4.html.

Hodapp, Christopher and Kannon, Alice von. *The Templar Code for Dummies*. Hoboken, NJ: Wiley Publishing Inc., 2007.

Jakobsson, Sverrir. 'Vinland and Wishful Thinking Medieval and Modern Fantasies'. *Canadian Journal of History/Annales canadiennes d'histoire* 47 (2012), pp. 493–514.

Juengst, E.T., Fishman, J.R., McGowan, M.L. and Settersten, R.A. Jr. 'Serving Epigenetics before Its Time'. *Trends in Genetics* 30 (2014), pp. 427–9.

Kapell, Matthew Wilhelm and Elliott, Andrew B.R. 'Introduction: To Build a Past that Will "Stand the Test of Time" – Discovering Historical Facts, Assembling Historical Narratives'. In *Playing with the Past: Digital Games and the Simulation of History*, ed. Matthew Wilhelm Kapell and Andrew B.R. Elliott. New York: Bloomsbury, 2013, pp. 1–30.

Kaplan, Jeffrey. 'Nothing Is True, Everything Is Permitted: Premodern Religious Terrorism'. *Terrorism and Political Violence* 31 (2019), pp. 1076–80.

Kaufman, Amy S. and Grewell, Cory. 'Blood Will Out: Genealogy as Destiny in Medieval(ist) Gaming'. In *Neomedievalism in the Media: Essays on Film, Television, and Electronic Games*, ed. Carol L. Robinson and Pamela Clements. Lewiston: The Edwin Mellen Press, 2012, pp. 283–306.

Kim, Dorothy. 'White Supremacists Have Weaponized an Imaginary Viking Past. It's Time to Reclaim the Real History'. *Time*, 15 April 2019. https://time.com/5569399/viking-history-white-nationalists/.

Komel, Mirt. 'Orientalism in *Assassin's Creed:* Self-Orientalizing the Assassins from Forerunners of Modern Terrorism into Occidentalized Heroes'. *Teorija in Praksa* 51 (2014), pp. 72–90.

Komel, Mirt. 'Re-orientalizing the Assassins in Western Historical-Fiction Literature Orientalism and Self-Orientalism in Bartol's *Alamut*, Tarr's *Alamut*, Boschert's *Assassins of Alamut* and Oden's *Lion of Cairo*'. *European Journal of Cultural Studies* 17 (2014), pp. 525–48.

Lewis, Bernard. 'The Sources for the History of the Syrian Assassins'. *Speculum* 27 (1952), pp. 475–89.

Lewis, Bernard. *The Assassins: A Radical Sect in Islam*. London: Phoenix, 2003.

Lyons, Matthew N. 'Ctrl-Alt-Delete: The Origins and Ideology of the Alternative Right'. *Political Research Associates*, 20 January 2017. https://politicalresearch.org/2017/01/20/ctrl-alt-delete-report-on-the-alternative-right#toc-executive-summary.

Migicovsky, Zoe and Igor Kovalchuk. 'Epigenetic Memory in Mammals'. *Frontiers in Genetics* 2 (2011), pp. 1–7.

Moss, Richard. '*Assassin's Creed*: An Oral History'. *Polygon*, 3 October 2019. https://www.polygon.com/features/2018/10/3/17924770/assassins-creed-an-oral-history-patrice-desilets.

Perry, David. 'White supremacists love Vikings. But they've got history all wrong.' *The Washington Post*, 31 May 2017. https://www.washingtonpost.com/posteverything/wp/2017/05/31/white-supremacists-love-vikings-but-theyve-got-history-all-wrong/.

Picknett, Lynn and Prince, Clive. *The Templar Revelation: Secret Guardians of the True Identity of Christ*. London: Transworld Publishers, 1997.

Rothstein, Mark A., Cai, Yu and Marchant, Gary E. 'The Ghost in Our Genes: Legal and Ethical Implications of Epigenetics'. *Health Matrix Clevel* 19 (2009), pp. 1–62. https://www.ncbi.nlm.nih.gov/pmc/articles/PMC3034450/.

Serwer, Adam. 'White Nationalisms' Deep American Roots'. *The Atlantic*, April 2019. https://www.theatlantic.com/magazine/archive/2019/04/adam-serwer-madison-grant-white-nationalism/583258/.

Shahid, Natasha. 'Sectarianist Writings in Islam: Prejudice against the Hashashin in 12th and 13th Century Muslim Historiography'. *International Journal of Arts & Sciences* 9 (2016), pp. 437–48.

Shaw, Adrienne. 'The Tyranny of Realism: Historical Accuracy and Politics of Representation in *Assassin's Creed III*'. *Loading... The Journal of the Canadian Game Studies Association* 9 (2014), pp. 4–24.

Smarandache, Bogdan. 'The Franks and the Nizari Isma'ilis in the Early Crusade Period'. *Al-Masaq* 24 (2012), pp. 221–39.

Sora, Steven. *The Lost Treasures of the Knights Templar: Solving the Oak Island Mystery*. Rochester, Vermont: Destiny Books, 1999.

Ubisoft. 'Ubisoft Announces Outstanding Sales Performance for *Assassin's Creed*™ and Raises Guidance for Fiscal 2007–08'. https://web.archive.org/web/20071218091159/http://www.ubi.com/US/News/Info.aspx?nId=5017.

Virani, Shafique N. *The Ismailis in the Middle Ages: A History of Survival, a Search for Salvation*. Oxford: Oxford University Press, 2007.

Wallace-Murphy, Tim and Hopkins, Marilyn. *Templars in America: From the Crusades to the New World*. New York: Barnes & Noble, 2004.

Westin, Jonathan and Hedlund, Ragnar. 'Polychronia – Negotiating the Popular Representation of a Common Past in *Assassin's Creed*'. *Journal of Gaming and Virtual Worlds* 8 (2016), pp. 3–20.

Wilson, Ian. *The Turin Shroud: The Burial Cloth of Jesus Christ?* New York: Image Books, 1979.

Index

Note: *Italic* page numbers refer to figures and page numbers followed by "n" denote endnotes.

For Product Safety Concerns and Information please contact our EU
representative GPSR@taylorandfrancis.com
Taylor & Francis Verlag GmbH, Kaufingerstraße 24, 80331 München, Germany

www.ingramcontent.com/pod-product-compliance
Lightning Source LLC
LaVergne TN
LVHW011030110826
845149LV00015B/3355

* 9 7 8 1 0 3 2 8 7 8 5 7 7 *